the series on school reform

Patricia A. Wasley   Ann Lieberman   Joseph P. McDonald
Bank Street College of Education   NCREST   New York University

SERIES EDITORS

Central Park East and Its Graduates:
"Learning by Heart"
   DAVID BENSMAN

Taking Charge of Curriculum:
Teacher Networks and Curriculum
Implementation
   JÁCOB E. ADAMS, JR.

Teaching With Power: Shared Decision-
Making and Classroom Practice
   CAROL REED

Good Schools / Real Schools: Why School
Reform Doesn't Last
   DEAN FINK

Beyond Formulas in Mathematics and
Teaching: Dynamics of the High School
Algebra Classroom
   DANIEL CHAZAN

School Reform Behind the Scenes
   JOSEPH P. McDONALD, THOMAS HATCH,
   EDWARD KIRBY, NANCY AMES,
   NORRIS M. HAYNES, AND EDWARD T.
   JOYNER

Looking Together at Student Work: A
Companion Guide to *Assessing Student
Learning*
   TINA BLYTHE, DAVID ALLEN, AND
   BARBARA SHIEFFELIN POWELL

Teachers—Transforming Their World and
Their Work
   ANN LIEBERMAN AND LYNNE MILLER

Teaching in Common: Challenges to Joint
Work in Classrooms and Schools
   ANNE DiPARDO

Charter Schools:
Another Flawed Educational Reform?
   SEYMOUR B. SARASON

Assessing Student Learning: From
Grading to Understanding
   DAVID ALLEN, EDITOR

Racing with the Clock: Making Time
for Teaching and Learning in School Reform
   NANCY E. ADELMAN,
   KAREN PANTON WALKING EAGLE, AND
   ANDY HARGREAVES, EDITORS

The Role of State Departments of
Education in Complex School Reform
   SUSAN FOLLETT LUSI

Making Professional Development Schools
Work: Politics, Practice, and Policy
   MARSHA LEVINE AND
   ROBERTA TRACHTMAN, EDITORS

How It Works—Inside a School–College
Collaboration
   SIDNEY TRUBOWITZ AND PAUL LONGO

Surviving School Reform: A Year in the Life
of One School
   LARAINE K. HONG

Eyes on the Child: Three Portfolio Stories
   KATHE JERVIS

Revisiting "The Culture of the
School and the Problem of Change"
   SEYMOUR B. SARASON

Teacher Learning:
New Policies, New Practices
   MILBREY W. McLAUGHLIN AND
   IDA OBERMAN, EDITORS

What's Happening in Math Class?:
Envisioning New Practices Through
Teacher Narratives (Volume 1)
   DEBORAH SCHIFTER, EDITOR

What's Happening in Math Class?:
Reconstructing Professional Identities
(Volume 2)
   DEBORAH SCHIFTER, EDITOR

Reaching for a Better Standard: English
School Inspection and the Dilemma of
Accountability for American Public Schools
   THOMAS A. WILSON

(Continued)

the series on school reform, *continued*

This series also incorporates earlier titles in the Professional Development and Practice Series

Central Park East and Its Graduates

"LEARNING BY HEART"

David Bensman

Foreword by Deborah Meier

Teachers College, Columbia University
New York and London

Published by Teachers College Press, 1234 Amsterdam Avenue, New York, NY 10027

Library of Congress Cataloging-in-Publication Data

Bensman, David, 1949–
    Central Park East and its graduates : learning by heart / David Bensman ; foreword by Deborah Meier.
       p.   cm. — (The series on school reform)
    Includes bibliographical references and index.
    ISBN 0-8077-3993-6 (cloth : alk. paper)—ISBN 0-8077-3992-8 (pbk. : alk. paper)
    1. Central Park East Elementary School (New York, N.Y.) 2. Urban schools—New York (State)—New York—Case studies. 3. Minorities—Education—New York (State)—New York—Case studies. I. Title. II. Series.
    LD7501.N5 B545 2000
    372.9747'1—dc21   00-056374

ISBN 0-8077-3992-8 (paper)
ISBN 0-8077-3993-6 (cloth)

Printed on acid-free paper
Manufactured in the United States of America

07 06 05 04 03 02 01 00   8 7 6 5 4 3 2 1

Contents

Foreword

THERE ARE FEW long-range accounts of the impact of precollegiate schooling on our lives. Even biographies and autobiographies offer little evidence of reflections. Given the number of years so many people—especially of the class of people who write books—spend in school and the presumed importance of schooling in our intellectual development, this omission seems peculiar. More is noted about the influence of particular teachers—this or that person who made a difference in our life. But not schools. It's as though school days were best forgotten, except for that notable exception—dear old Mrs. So-and-So.

There is one class of books that defy this generalization—books about noteworthy English elite public (private) schools, and a few histories of noteworthy American private schools. Boarding schools, imbued with the power to shape the leadership of a nation, are remembered for their institutional cultures, each proudly different, special. The exception itself offers us some possible explanations, and sets the stage for thinking about David Bensman's story of Central Park East.

Our ordinary public schools were not intended to "shape" the nation beyond giving its members some rudimentary social, civic, and academic skills. Their task was to impart neutral mechanical "skills"—handwriting and being on time, and neutral knowledge—the capitals and rivers, and how to spell and do multiplication tables. For such tasks one school was not intended to be much different from another. Teachers and schools were expected to be interchangeable, offspring of a single stripped-down model. Anything else smacked of interfering in the task of home and community. Ordinary public schools were decidedly not for the "rearing" of the young, as were the elite schools of the land—the public schools were just for schooling. This interchangeability also was used to explain the absence of any provision for parental choice between schools—which were all much alike.

Thus Central Park East is a frankly different creature—and was from its inception. We began it with various private school models in our heads.

We wanted to rear a different, more universal kind of elite—to give the kids who came to our school a taste of what it might be like to see themselves as the possessors of "wonderful ideas" (in Eleanor Duckworth's felicitous phrase), makers of things and inventors of their own lives. We wanted them to care about each other, and by extension their fellow beings throughout their lives. We wanted them to care about the world and do something in it. And we were pretty frank and aboveboard about this. We not only didn't think it would conflict with their learning to spell and know the names of the states, we even suspected that over the long haul it would contribute to such knowledge and skill. In a democracy, we argued that everyone must be the shaper of the nation.

We didn't *want* to be seen as interchangeable, or even replicable in the usual sense. And we weren't trying to be just a collection of great individual teachers. We saw ourselves as a community that, year after year, would speak in a common voice about what matters. But what we said might not be the same as the school next door. We didn't want a narrow "party line," but we had a somewhat specific viewpoint about a great many things, which separated us from others. As long as we didn't hide this viewpoint, we thought it a grand thing for children to grow up amid such a collection of strong-minded adults. The one worry we had was whether families would feel included or excluded by such a teacher-dominated adult community. We knew—intellectually—that unless the whole family bought into our work and school, it would fail. But finding the ways to include the family respectfully came hard. We knew that food and good times were a part of it. The easier part. But including the family's agenda—even where it differed from ours—came more painfully. We struggled with it.

Reading David Bensman's account of the school as seen through the eyes of young adults, and in some cases their parents, 10 years after they had left the school, is stunning. It seems we did better with families than we often feared at the time, or perhaps they were more generous about our failings in retrospect. Whenever we get discouraged about our insistence on building the strengths of children, our nurturing their peculiar and even oddball interests and passion, we need to reread this book. When we are told it is sentimental to count so heavily on the importance of building strong bonds between peers and between generations, rereading these accounts gives us new determination. It's why we're such crazy fanatics about small schools where everyone not only knows each other but can be heard, can be a mover and shaker.

In our new elementary school in Boston, these stories are critical to our work. We're living through a time when, in a new incarnation called "standards," the interchangeable-parts mentality has reemerged with great power (even as the idea of letting public schooling die off entirely has gained ground). The one-best-practice and one-best-curriculum are seen by some as the only savior for the most vulnerable children—the children of the poor. At such a moment Bensman's book is doubly valuable. The recognition that schools—as communities—offer hope and possibility, and intellectual competence, especially for those families who live lives of quiet despair, is particularly needed. Children have never been reared in more anonymous and estranged settings—divorced from the adult communities that they might play a useful role in. They have fewer and fewer contacts with any genuine communities beyond immediate families and like-minded peers, and voracious media that feed their narrowest narcissism. The sheer neighborliness that once went with public schools—even the interchangeable ones—no longer comes naturally. Schools must literally help create communities, rather than expect to live off them.

But strong and idiosyncratic public schools, each different from the others, could offer to all young people what Central Park East offered these youngsters. That more than 100 offspring schools have been born in New York City, carrying out the CPE idea in their own often very different ways, suggests there's a hunger for such schools and people prepared to organize them. It could be . . .

David Bensman has brought them alive to us in a way that few researchers could do. He allowed himself to get to know these youngsters, not to ask them a set of pollster questions. He was prepared to set aside any agenda of his own to hear their agenda. He therefore listened also to their struggles with life outside of schools and reminds us how much of an impact those struggles had on the way schools worked. He also allowed himself to listen to the role their families played, and these interviews led him to interview some of their families as well. What emerges is a story not just of one particular group of students from one particular school, but also a picture of what it was (and probably still is) like to grow up in East Harlem in the latter half of the twentieth century.

Deborah Meier

Acknowledgments

A LONGITUDINAL STUDY like this one can be done only if it is supported by many people and organizations. Several people worked with me virtually every step of the way, helping me to ask the right questions, to extract meaning from the data, and to develop my arguments. In particular, the collaboration of Kathe Jervis, Jon Snyder, Alice Seletsky, Deborah Meier, and Linda Fitzgerald contributed immensely to this effort, and I owe them all a great intellectual and personal debt.

I was fortunate to have had help from a large number of friends, colleagues, and assistants. To each of the following people, I would like to express my thanks and appreciation:

Jane Andrias, Carla Ascher, William Ayers, Sal Barcia, Connie Brady, John Burton, Carmen Cabello, Patricia Carini, Janet Carter, Ted Chittenden, Malik Coleman, Tishuanda Cunningham, Pam Cushing, Linda Darling-Hammond, Steve Director, Adrienne Eaton, Priscilla Ellington, Brenda Engel, Michelle Fine, Digna Galarza, Manuel Garrido, Areli Gonazales, Mark Gordon, Jessica Govea, Stephanie Harriet, Kyle Haver, Charles Heckscher, Aurea Hernandez, Nancy Hoffman, Tracy Huff, Ruth Jordan, Bruce Kanze, Jeffrey Katz, William Kornblum, Estelle Kramer, Sheila Lamb, Heather Lewis, Ann Lieberman, Maritza Macdonald, Amalia Marchitto, Lucy Matos, Joseph McDonald, Peggy McMullen, Bruce McPherson, Mae Miller, Carolyn Montanez, Carol Mulligan, Donna Muncey, Gail O'Brien, Sondra Perl, Jean Rojas, Mike Rose, Susan Schurman, Russell Seymour, Yvonne Smith, Barry Soloway, Paul Tainsh, Vivian Wallace, Jonathan Wentz, Gita Wilder, Nancy Wilson, and Nicky Wolfe.

In addition, I would like to thank the CPE graduates and their parents for their cooperation. I owe them a great debt; what they taught me will forever be part of me.

The entire staff of the Center for Collaborative Education supported my work in innumerable ways, large and small, and I thank each of them.

I would like also to thank the staff of the National Center for Restructuring Education, Schools, and Teaching for their help preparing this manuscript for publication. While many at NCREST have been named above, I'd like to add the name of Diane Harrington, whose gentle editing worked wonders.

At Teachers College Press, I've enjoyed working with Catherine Bernard and Carole Saltz, whose editorial suggestions helped me shorten the manuscript and make it more readable.

Finally, I'd like to thank Henry Drewry and the Andrew W. Mellon Foundation, as well as the Exxon Foundation and the Spencer Foundation for their research support. The School of Management and Labor Relations at Rutgers University, as well as the Department of Labor Studies and Employment Relations, provided crucial support and encouragement as well.

Introduction

THIS STORY BEGAN in 1974, when the Central Park East (CPE) Elementary School in East Harlem was organized to offer a very different approach to educating minority children in urban schools. Those who made up the Central Park East family asked what seemed radical questions:

- What would happen if we gave students in urban schools the best education American society knew how to offer?
- What would happen if we created a school in East Harlem modeled after the best private schools?
- Could we run such a school on the limited resources available to urban public schools?
- Could a school based on such different theories of teaching and learning, and structured in such a divergent manner, survive within a centralized school system?
- What would happen if instead of requiring students to be more rigidly tracked or imposing standardized curricula from the top, we asked, Why not the best for the country's most needy children?

For 25 years, CPE has defied conventional wisdom. In heterogeneous classrooms, its staff has implemented the progressive educational practices previously the nearly exclusive province of private and suburban schools. In effect, CPE has challenged the notion that poor children cannot learn, that unless poverty is abolished, the disadvantaged are doomed to lives on welfare or in routinized workplaces. Many CPE students represent a population of American society that typically is given little and, what's more, expected to do little in an academic environment. The founders of CPE, however, not only do not accept that idea, but continually refute it through their innovative pedagogical approaches.

While many other progressive education reform efforts have fallen out of the mainstream, the collaborative efforts of a group of teachers, parents, and students in East Harlem have taken root and matured, capturing the attention of the district, city, and, eventually, the nation. But when those who know CPE best—students, parents, teachers—sing the praises of the school, they virtually never mention its national reputation or sustained rates of excellent academic achievement. Instead, in remembering the influence of CPE and the ways in which it has shaped their lives, CPE graduates and their parents tell stories of supportive learning communities, of personal growth in a variety of areas, of lasting relationships, and of life-long lessons. Indeed, then, their stories testify not to the success of CPE in the typical sense of the word, but to the way CPE has forged a *new* definition of success in education—one that inspires children in the classroom and beyond.

HISTORY OF THE PROJECT

I first was afforded the opportunity to investigate the CPE "phenomenon" in 1986, when the New York Community Trust, intrigued by CPE's reputation, commissioned and generously funded a history of the school's first 10 years. Motivated by my own curiosity, I proposed to work on the project when I heard that Deborah Meier, the school's founder, was looking for someone to quickly finish the overdue study.

The result was *Quality Education in the Inner City* (Bensman, 1987), which identified two keys to Central Park East's success. The first involved its philosophy of education. "Unlike almost all schools in America," I wrote, "CPE begins not with what outside experts have predetermined that the students need to learn, but with the students' own ideas and interests. The staff listen carefully to what children are saying and observe what they are doing. But most important, they respect those thoughts and actions" (p. 8). Respect was crucial not only in teacher–student relationships, but in administrator–teacher relationships, and school–family relationships as well. "By demonstrating consistent respect for children, parents and teachers, the CPE schools are able to get the best from all three—teachers give more of their time and devotion, children give more of their energy, parents give more of their concern" (p. 9).

But CPE's educational outlook was clearly not enough to explain the school's success, I argued, for a close reading of the school's history indicated that it had made many mistakes, including some that generated internal conflict severe enough to call the school's continued existence into question. What made CPE unusual, I argued, was it had survived its predictable mistakes and had done so for three reasons: It started small; it enjoyed staunch support from District 4 Superintendent Anthony Alvarado; and most teachers and parents felt that they had made such a large investment in the school's success that they wanted to give it a chance to grow and improve.

Before *Quality Education* was published, CPE's reputation grew exponentially as a result of Deborah Meier's winning the MacArthur "Genius" Award in the spring of 1986. Using the prize money she won, Meier founded the Center for Collaborative Education and began sending *Quality Education* to those expressing interest in school reform.

Ironically, at the time I wrote *Quality Education* in 1986, I did not consider it the full-out study it could have been—after all, the project was already behind schedule when I came aboard. Yet, here I was, hearing from people all over the country how helpful this study was proving to their efforts to improve local schools.

The magnitude of this response made me realize that the school reform effort was engaging the dedicated effort and concerted attention of people concerned with social justice, and I began to wonder about how I could aid their efforts. The chance came in 1991, when Deborah Meier proposed that I follow up on the early graduates of CPE, to evaluate the school's long-term impact on their school careers and personal lives.

Deborah's proposal appealed to me because writing *Quality Education in the Inner City* had not satisfied my curiosity about CPE's success. I knew what CPE's staff had done to reach their students, but I didn't really understand how. How could a teacher keep track of what 30 students were thinking and doing? How could a teacher encourage and nourish such a large and diverse group of children? Finally, what did quality education mean to inner-city students in the long term? Would the strengths gained in nurturing classrooms enable students to overcome challenges posed by broken families, poverty, and discrimination?

When Deborah first proposed that I track student achievement over time, it seemed like a simple proposition. I designed a study comprising two parts: The first would be a phone survey to gather mostly quantitative data; the second would be in-depth interviews of a subset of the graduates to ask them to expand on comments they made in the phone survey. As is usually the case, though, researching the real world proved unimaginably complicated.

Antiquated Board of Education records made even the first part of the study a chore. Finding most of the hard data, such as grades, standardized test scores, attendance records, and Regents examination results, was nearly impossible. While I did not believe that these quantitative measures could accurately gauge CPE's impact, I was prepared to use such data in order to respond to those skeptics who distrusted anecdotal evidence and demanded "hard evidence." Unfortunately, even responding to such skeptics proved more difficult than I had anticipated.

Failing to find most of this hard evidence from the Board of Education, we decided to obtain the data from the students—a task that once again proved easier said than done. With the help of Jean Rojas and Digna Galarza, two long-time CPE staff members who lived in East Harlem, I was able to locate, over the course of 2 years, the phone numbers of 117 of the 135 members of CPE's first 6 graduating classes (1978–1983). Some graduates were easy to find; they lived at the same address, or they still came to visit former teachers, or they had younger brothers or sisters still in the school. But other graduates proved more elusive. Some had moved but they, or their relatives, still lived in the neighborhood; when Jean or Digna ran into those graduates, their phone numbers would be jotted down and added to the list. Other graduates were traced because someone at CPE, usually Jean or Digna, remembered that so-and-so was so-and-so's cousin, or such-and-such's mother was best friends with so-and-so. Eventually, as I began surveying graduates, they told me the whereabouts of former classmates, some as far away as Florida, Puerto Rico, Texas, and California.

Of course, possessing the correct telephone numbers did not guarantee success. As anyone who's ever dodged a phone solicitor knows, there are more enjoyable ways to spend an evening than answering survey questions, simple as they may be. For young men and women, restless and on the move, or saddled with work and family responsibilities, returning the phone call of a stranger was not a high priority. Although I kept reminding myself that there were sensible reasons why I couldn't reach some graduates or why they wouldn't call me back, I couldn't help but grow discouraged as my prime hours for phoning—7 p.m. to 9 p.m.—would pass without my reaching one graduate.

What kept me going were the times I reached graduates eager to talk about CPE. As they answered my questions about where they lived, and where they'd gone to school, they began to tell me about how much CPE had meant to their lives, how much they remembered about their teachers and classmates, how glad they were to be back in touch, even indirectly, and how they definitely had to go back to visit.

And then there were the conversations, equally interesting, with those graduates whose memories of CPE were less than idyllic. Usually, their opinions were harder to elicit; those critical of CPE assumed I didn't want to hear their views, or else they feared that their negative comments would get back to somebody. Earnestly, I would insist that everyone's opinions were important, that I had an open mind, that I would respect everybody's privacy. Usually my reassurances worked, but sometimes it took months to convince critics to open up.

Completing the survey proved to be the easy part of the job; interviewing a subset of the graduates in depth challenged my resolve even more than the survey. I remember vividly my first attempted interview, with Shelley Bailey. When I'd called Shelley to arrange the interview, she told me she was joining the Navy in a few days, so we'd have to meet the day before she was due to report. As I drove from my home in the New Jersey suburbs to Shelley's home in Central Harlem, I listened once again to the recorded telephone survey we'd done the year before. "Once I got to CPE I felt very comfortable. I remember when it was time to leave, I didn't want to go. I just wished that CPE would never end." As I heard Shelley's voice describing how she'd loved her elementary school, my anticipation soared.

My high was short-lived, however, as I walked to the building's entrance, pressed the buzzer to Shelley's apartment, and nothing happened. Shelley never showed up.

My second attempted interview didn't go much better. Natasha Blake, who lived on 112th Street below Morningside Park, wasn't home when I arrived either.

By now, I was considering abandoning my efforts to do the in-depth interviews. After all, I had completed a lot of the phone surveys. Surely I could say *something* significant about CPE graduates.

But a week later, when I called Natasha again, she was apologetic. She'd been in the recording studio, she told me, it got late, she lost track of the time. And when she got home, she had to put her son to bed, so she forgot to call me. "All right," I thought, "I'll give it one more try."

When I met Natasha, I forgot all my frustrations. Natasha remembered classroom events in vivid detail, recalled all her teachers, all her classmates. And she emphatically believed that her time at CPE had shaped her subsequent school experiences, her personality, parenting, and musical career.

Furthermore, as Natasha and I shared our feelings about her neighborhood and compared our experiences raising toddlers (my son was 4 years old at the time), I realized that this was going to be more than a fascinating academic project about other people; the research process forced me to rethink my ideas of who I am, what I do, and how I am connected to others.

The interview process also forced me to rethink my research design. Talking to Steve Hernandez one day in his family's apartment high above the roofs of East Harlem's tenements, I asked Steve how he had ended up at CPE when he lived across the street from a different elementary school. Steve didn't know.

Then, Steve's father came home, introduced himself, and sat down to see what was happening. When I explained that Steve couldn't tell me why he'd gone to CPE, Mr. Hernandez took over. Years before, he told me, he'd been "active in the community." As a member of the Young Lords, a revolutionary Puerto Rican nationalist organization, he had become acquainted with a teacher in the bilingual program of the neighborhood school, and she had recommended CPE.

Since Steve had described his father as a "handyman" who did odd jobs fixing cars and selling things in the neighborhood, his father's story took me aback. Clearly there was a dimension to CPE that my work had not revealed up to this point—the culture, values, and expectations of the families that chose to send their children to CPE. Quickly I applied to the Spencer Foundation, requesting funds to supplement my research with interviews of the graduates' parents. When Spencer agreed to provide these funds, I began exploring the relationship between the culture of the families and the culture of the school.

Now as my son Joseph begins sixth grade, I have come to see the school–family relationship as being of crucial importance, not only for educational research, but for me as a parent who wants the best for my boy. As I explored the personal issues provoked by my encounters with CPE graduates, I began to understand the data I was collecting differently than I would have earlier. My survey data demonstrate that CPE graduates achieved high rates of school progress compared with public school students of comparable socioeconomic backgrounds. But I no longer view this finding as the most important outcome of the study.

When the graduates themselves assessed how their elementary school experience contributed to their lives, they rarely limited themselves to academics; indeed, they cited gains in their emotional strength and social skills as prominently as they did school progress. Furthermore, the graduates described academic progress as being inseparable from emotional and social growth. Over and over again, students told me that their teachers provided the support and encouragement they needed to discover an interest and develop a skill; in turn, their self-esteem improved and they took on greater academic challenges.

In effect, students told me that if I want to explain their high rates of academic achievement, I must look at the school as more than an academic environment. Rather, I should examine it as a learning community where adults structured the relationships between adults and children, and among the students, in order to foster the students' academic, emotional, *and* social growth.

Moreover, students told me that CPE's success had to be measured by more than graduation rates. By attending CPE, graduates told me, they'd become stronger, better people than they would have become otherwise; they'd become better citizens and employees, stronger, happier, more open and self-confident; they'd gained an appreciation of diverse people and cultures, an ability to take advantage of more of society's resources; they'd learned how to get along with others and solve interpersonal disputes without recourse to scapegoating and violence. In short, graduates told me that CPE offered a solution not only to America's educational dilemmas, but to many of its social problems as well.

The results of my study appeared as *Lives of the Graduates of the Central Park East Elementary School: What Did They Do? What Did They Learn?* (Bensman, 1994). As the manuscript began to take form, I shared it with others, including my colleagues at Rutgers University.

My colleagues' feedback proved helpful. While almost all of them seemed persuaded that CPE had had a strong impact on its graduates, they pressed me to go further in explaining the school's success. The key question, posed most sharply by Charles Heckscher, then chair of the Department of Labor Studies and Employment Relations, was, "Why had Central Park East achieved success when so many similar progressive school reform efforts had failed?"

Charles's question prompted me to revisit my earlier history of the school. As I reread my narrative, I realized that much of what had made CPE successful was not part of the original blueprint, but instead was created by teachers as they identified problems and searched for solutions. Suddenly, what stood out was less CPE's grounding in progressive theory, and more the organization's ability to learn and grow.

This dimension of the CPE story had been missing from the graduates' accounts because, as children, they had not been aware of the ways their school had changed over time. And so, I decided, if I wanted to tell the full story, I would have to write another manuscript, one combining the graduates' perspective about what helped them learn with an analysis of how CPE developed the capacity to invent the practices that helped students learn. This analysis of CPE's organizational development makes clear that CPE's success involved overcoming past major mistakes, improving on inadequate theories and practices, and developing new capacities unimagined at the time of the school's establishment.

OVERVIEW OF BOOK

To accomplish this investigation, the book is organized into seven chapters. Chapter 1 presents the data outlining CPE graduates' academic achievement. Chapter 2 examines the academic pathways constructed by students and teachers to enable graduates to succeed. This chapter considers as well the graduates who dissented from the consensus view. Chapter 3 examines how graduates drew on the caring relationships fostered by CPE to create pathways to emotional and social growth.

Since CPE's diversity made it unusual among progressive elementary schools, Chapter 4 considers how CPE was able to bridge racial and cultural divides, and, especially, how the "integrationist" ethic of CPE's founders flourished in a world where integration as a social ideal was losing its luster.

While CPE was established by teachers searching to put their own ideas about teaching and learning into action, the role of parents as partners increased steadily. In Chapter 5, parents of graduates describe not only why they chose to send their children to CPE but also how their initial enthusiasm for the school propelled them to support it through political action and fund raising as well as educational support activities. In this chapter, the parents' enthusiasm for CPE's programs challenges some of our initial assumptions about parental resistance to progressive education.

Graduates talk in Chapter 6 about what they are doing now and what they hope to do in the future. As they describe their triumphs and setbacks, their hopes and dreams for themselves and their children, some of whom are now entering elementary school themselves, graduates testify that CPE's founders successfully passed on their legacy—a belief in the dignity of the individual and the value of cooperative effort; commitment to social equality and cultural diversity; and respect for the human spirit's creativity and the American citizen's communal responsibility.

Finally, the concluding chapter considers CPE's significance for contemporary efforts to improve America's public schools. In particular, CPE's organizational strengths as a learning community are examined with reference to contemporary literature about how institutions restructure themselves in the name of continuous improvement. The final section probes how our understanding of organizational change in one school not only can help shape our strategy for improving public education for all America's children, but can help us think through how to improve universities and other institutions that need to learn how to learn.

I leave the last word to a member of CPE's staff, Alice Seletsky. I asked Alice to write an Afterword reflecting on what participating in and reading this study of the CPE effort has meant to her, as she makes sense of her long career in public education. Alice's essay exemplifies the habits of mind that made CPE's staff successful—the relentless refusal to accept partial answers, the persistent determination to seek better solutions, the restless inventiveness that finds a way to incorporate accidental discoveries into systemic improvements.

Over the years, these habits of mind have challenged me, inspired me, and finally driven me to apply what I have learned from CPE to my own chosen sphere, the university. As I have struggled to make my own department a learning organization, I have come to appreciate all the more the achievements of Alice, Debbie, Bruce, Digna, Jean, and the entire CPE community.

Searching for Meaning in the Survey Data

I STILL REMEMBER how skeptical I felt when I first heard about Central Park East Elementary School more than 20 years ago. It was then fashionable in my world to argue that America's urban schools could not be improved substantially until racism and poverty were eliminated. We thought that the activists organizing "open classrooms" and "free schools" were bound to be disappointed.

And we were not entirely wrong. Many of those efforts *were* abandoned. Others were absorbed within central public education systems. A few survived as private schools separate and apart from the public schools. Over all, progressive education reform efforts lost momentum, as they had done a generation earlier, in the 1940s.

With this history in mind, the quantitative results of my 1991 phone survey of CPE graduates seemed all the more surprising to me. From my phone calls to the 117 graduates we had tracked down, I determined that an impressive 94.8% of those I reached had graduated from high school or received a general equivalency diploma (GED), and almost two-thirds had enrolled in college.

But what did these numbers mean? While impressive on paper, did these results address the fears of parents, critics, and skeptics that CPE's brand of progressive education would produce students lacking in "basic skills," unable to make the transition to junior high school, and doomed to fail in high school or college? Or did they justify CPE's reputation as one of America's best public elementary schools?

DID CPE CREAM ITS STUDENT BODY?

Smug in my initial ideological certainty, I believed that the explanation for CPE's success was that the students were atypical—specially selected for success. Finding accurate meaning in my survey results, then, required that

I find an appropriate comparison group for CPE's graduates. If they were more like students at a select private school than like the public school population, if CPE selected only the most talented students from families highly motivated to support their children's success in school, the graduates' high rates of school achievement would not be surprising. On the other hand, if CPE's student body was typical of urban public schools, these rates would be remarkable. In short, I first needed to determine if CPE creamed the best students in order to achieve high rates of success.

Establishing a Comparison Group

To answer the creaming question, I compared CPE's students' demographic characteristics with those of a nonselective public school population. Because students came to Central Park East from all over New York City, rather than from East Harlem alone, I constructed a comparison between the demographic profile of the CPE graduates and that of the New York City public school population. The data used to make the comparison included race, household structure, parents' occupations, and family income (see Appendix A for data). For example, CPE's graduates are nearly 90% African American or Puerto Rican; these groups represent 70% of the New York City school population at the time.

Taken together, these comparative data refuted my initial hypothesis that CPE "creamed" when it selected its student body. The evidence indicates that CPE's population closely resembles that of the overall New York City public school population. If anything, CPE's population is skewed in the direction of increased risk of school failure.

Did CPE Grads Have Special Qualities?

Suggestive as these data are, a determined skeptic is not likely to be convinced. Given that CPE is a school of choice, the graduates' high rates of high school completion and college enrollment could be attributed to the special qualities possessed by the families that chose to send their children to this pioneering school. Did these families provide CPE students with unusual resources and support (Clark, 1983)?

While a retrospective study cannot answer that question conclusively, I began exploring it further by first determining whether the students I had located were representative of the graduates as a whole. In order to find out, I followed a procedure suggested by two researchers at Educational Testing Service, Edward Chittenden and Gita Wilder. I submitted 36 names, including the 18 we were unable to locate, and 18 others chosen at random from the group we had located, to a group of CPE teachers and asked them to

rate the students as having been "very likely to graduate high school and go
to college," "very unlikely to graduate high school and go to college," or
somewhere in the middle. When I compared the ratings of the two groups
of 18 names, they were identical, indicating that the 117 students about whom
we have data probably *are* representative of the population of graduates.

How Did CPE Admit Its Students?

One way to determine whether CPE students were special in a way hidden by demographic characteristics is to examine the school's admission
process. When CPE was established in 1974, the newly hired teachers
began visiting the Head Start and day care centers of East Harlem, posting
notices about their new "alternative school." At the same time, Digna
Galarza, a soon-to-be CPE staff member and long-time resident of East
Harlem, began spreading word of the new school to neighbors, friends, and
acquaintances in the Carver Houses, the New York City public housing
development where she lived, as well as to those on neighboring streets.

Budget cuts forced CPE to eliminate plans to open with a full-day kindergarten and a school bus to bring students from all over East Harlem to
the school. This meant that CPE had to draw its first student body from the
area of the neighborhood school, where pupil enrollment was declining.

In order to attract enough students to make the school viable, the
teachers were forced to change one of their basic premises. Instead of
admitting students only for kindergarten and first grade, they decided
to admit older children, especially older siblings of the kindergartners
and first graders.

Mrs. Ethel Powers, whose three children entered CPE in its second
year, remembers how CPE's first third/fourth-grade class came to be: "I
was so impressed that I wanted [my son] Jim to go. At that time, they only
had a first and second grade. So Debbie [Meier] said to me, 'If you can get
me at least nine students to start a third and fourth grade, I'll be glad to
take him.' So I hustled around. . . . I recruited seven or eight kids."

While Mrs. Powers heard about CPE from a teacher who felt it was
"equivalent to a private school," many parents were referred for a very
different reason: CPE was considered appropriate for children having difficulty in standard, "zoned" elementary schools. Children who had learning, behavioral, or emotional difficulties were all directed to alternative
schools. District 4 personnel recommended to parents that they consider
sending their children to CPE if they wanted to avoid "special schools" for
the learning disabled or the emotionally disturbed.

One mother remembers that before her daughter, Lola, enrolled at
CPE, she had been spending half her time in the Assistant Principal's of-

fice, as punishment for her constant fighting with classmates. Lola remembers suffering from family problems while at the school she attended before CPE.

> I remember things like my mom leaving [our apartment] and not knowing when she was coming back and then thinking it was my fault, not my father's. So I used to go to school and take that out on other people. . . . I guess I was rebelling, so I didn't sit down and I bothered the kids. . . . At CPE I had fun learning. I didn't want to beat up kids as much, because I wanted to do things.

A second mother sent her son to CPE because his elementary school wanted to get rid of him.

> Matthew had completed one year of kindergarten at the neighborhood school and he had just gone into first grade. He had a teacher who really needed the children to sit down and be quiet, and he was just not that kind of child. . . . He did have trouble with hitting and did have a wild raging temper. I think had he stayed at our neighborhood school, he would have quit school right then.

When told Matthew might have an easier time at CPE since it did not demand that students sit still in their chairs all day long, his mother seized the chance. "They understood that he had to move his muscles, and appreciated him for it. They just let him blossom."

In addition to those seeking "the equivalent of a private school" and those grasping at an alternative to special education programs, two other sources began to feed CPE. One was a group of progressive White parents who lived on the Upper East Side, near Central Park East. They had come together to organize a community-run nursery school in the Washington Houses, a public housing development on 97th Street and Second Avenue. According to Mrs. Wilson, "It was a private nursery school. At the time it was organized, there wasn't any Head Start. The organizers really wanted to have some place where their children could have a social educational experience. It was run by the parents."

Another group began sending their children to CPE from Central Harlem in the mid-1970s, although their link was fortuitous. Joseph DeSilver often subcontracted computer data processing work to Fred Meier, Deborah Meier's then-husband. Since Fred ran his business out of the basement of the Meier brownstone, DeSilver got to know the Meier family. Deborah Meier made an indelible impression on DeSilver in 1975, when budget cuts forced one of his principal clients, the New York City Board of Education, to delay payment on a contract. When DeSilver told Fred Meier that he would have to lay off his employees, Deborah Meier overheard and took out her check-book. "She gave me an unsecured loan for $5,000 so I could keep my business going. I didn't think anybody would do that." Later, when Mrs. Meier told DeSilver about Central Park East, he decided to send his children there, not so much because he agreed with Meier's educational philosophy but because he "felt sure that anyone who was as caring and generous as she was would have to be great for children. It was a matter of her character."

After the DeSilvers enrolled their children in CPE, they began telling their acquaintances with children at Champ Montessori school in West Harlem about the wonderful public school in East Harlem. This network brought 15 students to CPE in the years 1978–1983.

Thus several streams of students fed CPE in its early years—local Puerto Rican and African American parents looking for a better school, parents of children with learning or emotional difficulties, progressive White parents from the Upper East Side, and African American parents from Central Harlem who had sent their children to a Montessori school. These streams, plus parents drawn to the school through word of mouth, meant that by 1978 CPE had more applicants than it could admit.

To determine which applicants should be accepted, CPE did not test students, or review their grade reports; instead, it used a modified lottery system. In order to enroll at the CPE schools, parents must fill out an application. A complex lottery system then is used to select among the applicants, so that everyone has an equal chance.

According to a 1992 study of CPE I, the original Central Park East Elementary School,

> Children from the neighborhood are given first priority, and remaining ethnic slots (e.g., equal proportions of African-Americans, Latino-Americans, and "others") are filled by random drawing. When a child's name is drawn, all other siblings are automatically admitted to the school. At no point in the process, to the consternation of some applicants, is academic ability, socio-economic class, or political clout taken into account. . . . After a family's name is selected in the lottery, guardian and child are required to visit the school, and invited to spend a day there and have a personal conversation with the director. Observation guidelines are provided for their visit. If, at the end of this process, the family indicates that CPE I is the right environment for them, they become members of the CPE I community. (Snyder, Lieberman, Macdonald, & Goodwin, 1992, p. 92)

There are two exceptions to the process of random selection. First, children of the staff and siblings of attending students have always been admitted automatically. Second, in the early years, when a small number of slots opened up in the upper grades, applicants for these slots were invited to visit the school. Founding CPE Director Deborah Meier believes that when the schools chose among these applicants for the few slots in the upper grades, students with greater academic abilities may have been given preference.

Results of the Lottery System

What sort of student body did this complicated lottery system produce? Was it overwhelmingly a group of talented children, or children from unusually ambitious families?

If CPE's early students resemble its current ones, the answer is clearly no. Currently, more CPE students are eligible for special education services than are District 4 students as a whole (20% compared with 15%). These data are consistent with the school's philosophy: Believing that almost all children will be more successful at CPE than in available public alternatives, the school attempts to admit a cross-section of the public school population. For example:

Carmen San Jose was the second of five children born out of wedlock to a single mother. Carmen's grandparents were so unhappy about their daughter's teenage pregnancies that they would not allow her to live in their apartment, consigning her instead to a basement apartment in the same building. Carmen's mother did not work, subsisting largely on welfare. When Carmen was at CPE, she had major speech problems, suffered from seizures and asthma, and was acutely self-conscious about the thick lenses she wore to correct her weak vision. She says of herself then:

> I would do things to get attention, scream or pick a fight. I felt I was ugly looking. Not even a creature would speak to me and I didn't have many friends. . . . I had to do crazy things, so I could get attention.

Carmen received a GED, and has worked for 7 years as a secretary at the New York Housing Authority. She overcame her speech problems, wears contact lenses, has been cured of asthma, and no longer suffers from seizures. When interviewed, she was planning her wedding and preparing for a promotional exam administered by the New York City Civil Service system.

Amy Martinez was dyslexic. In her early years at CPE, she suffered from severe difficulty reading and writing. Amy left high school without earning her diploma. She is married, raising a young daughter, and taking care of her mentally challenged younger brother.

Kareem Walton suffered severe emotional difficulties. When he lost his temper, which was often, he would fly into uncontrollable rages. Kareem received intensive therapy, which allowed him to gain control of his temper. He completed a GED and worked for several years, but is currently out of work.

Anetta Peters, born in Central America, came to CPE speaking only Spanish. Had she stayed in her zoned elementary school, she would have been "sent to special ed" because of her reading difficulties. She graduated college with a nursing degree and is now employed as a registered nurse.

Tosha Prince's father joined a political sect and kidnapped her while she was in elementary school. Throughout the period Tosha was in elementary school, her mother was unwell.

> I think my mother really lost it, for a while anyway. . . . There was a period of time, from the time I was 9 years old, when she no longer had a real interest in my education or anything like that. . . . I just think she cracked. All the pressure that my father and his people put her under, with taking my brother and me and returning us and taking us and returning us, and the threatening phone calls and all that stuff pushed her over the edge. . . . She just suddenly had absolutely no ambition, no motivation, and it seemed like no concern for anything. It was very sad.

Tosha pursued a career as an actress after graduating from high school. When interviewed, she was attending City College, majoring in prelaw, and planning to be "Mayor of New York City."

Alfred Perez's father was shot and killed when he was a child. His mother was emotionally incapacitated during the time he was at CPE. Alfred completed high school, completed a training program in air conditioning repair, and got a job in his trade.

COMPARING THE GRADUATES

Keeping in mind the modified lottery system that CPE used to draw its students from a pool of applicants with diverse motivations and backgrounds, the question arises again: how to compare the CPE graduates' achievements with those of students who did not attend CPE?

The Graduates Compare

One informal approach I used was to ask CPE graduates and their parents how their school achievements compared with those of the neighborhood children with whom they had grown up. Those who lived in Central Harlem had mixed opinions: Mrs. Cartwright and her two children, both CPE graduates, said that they saw "a lot of young adults that are parents that are still living at home with their parents, not doing anything." But Jasmine Stevens, another CPE graduate who lived in the same middle-income housing complex as the Cartwrights, painted a more upbeat picture: "They're all in college. And it's weird, they all go to Black schools in the South."

The African American and Puerto Rican CPE graduates from East Harlem gave a more consistently negative assessment of how other young adults in their neighborhood were faring: Mary Law, who lived in a public housing project seven blocks from CPE during the time she attended the school, reported that while some of her old neighborhood girlfriends went to college, "the others are out of high school, and they're all mothers. They just stopped. They didn't know what they wanted. They didn't have that concern about what they were going to do." The girls she knew from CPE, on the other hand, were "all in college. They know what they want out of life." As for the boys in the neighborhood, her sister Cynthia, also a CPE graduate, reports that they "go sell drugs. It's peer pressure probably. They'll all be out there just trying to make a fast buck."

Steve Hernandez, who has lived in East Harlem all his life, agrees.

I have a sense of what most of the kids from around my neighborhood are doing. As far as I see, most of them are just into the streets, run drugs a lot. . . . They run drugs and some of them are even on it, some of them even use it.

Daniel Lopez, who grew up in the Carver Houses across the street from CPE, told a similar story.

Pretty much everybody who lived around my neighborhood, they went to the neighborhood school and there's nothing really to tell about them. I'm not going to say that it was a waste but they could have done a lot more with their lives than they are doing now. . . . These kids were out real late. They did basically whatever they wanted and most of their lives were spent hanging out.

Would You Send Your Own Children?

Another set of data that we may use indirectly to assess CPE's efficacy is the graduates' own subjective evaluation of the school. The graduates were asked, "If you had children, would you send them to Central Park East?" Seventy-seven (87.5%) answered "Yes"; eight (9.1%) answered "Yes, with some reservations"; and only three (3.4%) answered "No."

Evidence from Reading Tests

A third set of data, drawn from citywide reading tests, offers more quantitative evidence. These data from the 1970s and 1980s indicate that CPE students were substantially below national norms in second grade, but significantly exceeded those norms after they had attended the school for several years (Bensman, 1987).

TRANSITION TO SECONDARY SCHOOL

While the data on high school completion rates indicate that CPE graduates did far better than comparable New York City public school students, those data do not directly address the fears of some CPE parents that their children would leave CPE with weaknesses in "basic skills," with deficient general knowledge, and with poor study habits. Some parents feared that these deficiencies would make it difficult for their children to adjust to the demands of more traditional junior and senior high schools. To determine whether these predictions proved accurate, we asked students to list the strengths and weaknesses they brought with them to secondary school and how long it took to overcome the weaknesses.

Could They Overcome Weaknesses?

Overall, the students' reports did not justify their parents' concerns. Few students said that poor study habits (6%) or lack of "specific knowledge" (2%) proved to be problems in junior high school, and none said they had trouble meeting deadlines. Furthermore, while the two weaknesses most frequently reported, "spelling, punctuation" (17.4%) and "math skills" (36.0%), are precisely the ones parents worried about, the majority of students overcame whatever weaknesses they experienced in 2 years or less, by the end of eighth grade.

Eugene Davidson, a White CPE graduate from the Upper East Side, was a member of this group. When he entered junior high at the Academy of Environmental Sciences, he was "sorely deficient" in math and science. But by the end of seventh grade, Eugene had overcome these problems. He went to Brooklyn Technical High School, one of the city's select public high schools, where he majored in architecture, earned a score of 1240 on his Scholastic Achievement Test, and went on to Grinnell College, where he majored in psychology.

For Shari Montes, who grew up within East Harlem's Puerto Rican community, graduated from CPE, and went to nearby East Harlem Performing Arts Junior High School to study acting, "math, definitely math" was the weakness she had to overcome. It took her "about a year and a half." Then she went to John F. Kennedy High School, where, "honestly, I started off not so great," but over time, she began doing well. "I graduated with an 85 average. I just kept trying and trying and trying." Now Shari is at John Jay College, in New York City, planning to major in psychology so she can pursue the career she chose as a teenager—working with juvenile delinquents.

A smaller group of graduates, numbering 21 (42%) of those who answered this question, reported that it took them more than 2 years to overcome their weaknesses. If weaknesses that CPE graduates brought with them into junior high school impeded the academic progress of any students, we would expect it would be these 21. However, fully 18 of these 21 students eventually went to college. In fact, all but one of the 12 who said they never overcame their weaknesses at all went to college.

Marie Spain, another White student from the Upper East Side, is one of the three students who had long-lasting weaknesses and never went to college. "I always had a problem with math," she remembers. Marie's mother blames CPE for the problem, but Marie isn't so sure. "I had it when I was in a private school, with so-called wonderful teachers, and the problem didn't go away. I think it was my own learning disability." In high school, math stopped being a major problem for Marie, but "it was still not my best subject, ever."

Valerie Sanchez belongs to the group of CPE graduates who had a long-lasting weakness but went on to college anyway. Valerie "never did well" in social studies because she "wasn't interested." When I interviewed Valerie in her family's new home in Vega Baja, Puerto Rico, she elaborated:

> My trouble was always with social studies. . . . At Wagner Junior High School, it was terrible; it never interested me. In CPE, Alice involved me in many activities. I had to do many reports on other countries and many research projects. There was one where she got me involved in studying Iraq. In that case it was interesting. But once I got to junior high school, I totally lost it again. It got totally boring.

Did "Weak Skills" Keep Them Out of College?

In order to further analyze the data on weaknesses, I looked at each type of weakness, to determine if any typically were associated with low rates of college enrollment—none were. In fact, students who reported experiencing weaknesses in secondary school enrolled in college at a higher rate (84%) than did students reporting no weaknesses (76.5%). This suggests that students conscious of having had academic weaknesses may actually have had higher standards, or even been stronger students than those who said everything was okay.

CONCLUSION

If we accept that CPE's graduates came from socioeconomic backgrounds no more advantaged than those of the citywide public high school population, we can estimate that between 30 and 40 of the 111 CPE graduates who completed high school would not have done so had they followed the pattern of the citywide population; in addition, 20 CPE graduates who attended college would not have done so had they followed the pattern for all students citywide.

These estimates must be tempered: There may have been differences between CPE students and the citywide group that are not detectable using available measures, or, again, differences between the families of CPE students and those of the larger population may not be apparent from the comparative data.

Regardless of why the graduates' outcomes were superior to citywide averages, seven out of eight graduates said they would like to send their children to Central Park East.

These survey data told me that CPE's implementation of progressive educational theory did yield impressively high measurable rates of academic progress. But, of course, CPE was founded on the belief that success is not measured by grades, scores, or survey results. Since no 15-minute phone survey could tell me if CPE's program empowered its graduates to succeed outside the classroom, I began conducting in-person interviews of a subset of the graduates I had reached by phone. These interviews enabled me to trace the pathways CPE graduates followed not merely in their later academic endeavors, but in their long-term social and emotional growth as well.

ᔒ 2 ᔓ

Individual Pathways to Learning

Before I went to CPE in fifth grade, I was a mess because I hated school. I was going to a Lutheran school, The School on the Hill on 145th Street in Harlem. It was not a very fun place to be at all. During the third grade, I must have missed 2 weeks of school out of every month. I would get sick. My mother says I would actually come down with something legitimate, and I would have to stay home for a week or two. It never failed. . . .

Once I was at CPE, I would be so upset if I got sick and couldn't go to school. That's how much fun it was. You just got up and you looked forward to going to school. I had never, even in first and second grade [at the Modern School in Harlem], looked forward to going to school. CPE actually made it fun.

My teacher for fifth and sixth grade, Alice [Seletsky], was the sweetest person in the world. You didn't have somebody telling you, "You have to do this." You could make your way around the room at your own pace. If you liked to read, you could spend a little bit more time reading. Or if you liked math, you could do that. It was more like I was doing this on my own. It made you feel more independent and it gave you more confidence in yourself. My mother was pretty happy when she found that school.

(Kathy Title)

WHEN I BEGAN interviewing graduates like Kathy Title to find out what they remembered doing in elementary school, what activities they most enjoyed, what projects they were most proud of, what was difficult for them, or how they overcame their difficulties, they were often hesitant at first. But prompted with specific questions about what they had done in Leslie's second-grade classroom, or what it was they liked best about Alice, or what they thought of Barry's music program, most graduates, as did Kathy, brought up memories filled with vivid details.

What things helped me to learn? When I was in CPE, in sixth grade, Russ Seymour [the Assistant Director] got Tina Pittman and myself, the Two Musketeers, interested in reading poetry. It was Tina who first started this. Since we were always together, I did it [too], but I always had a feeling she was a little bit better at it than I was because I didn't really enjoy doing it too much. One day, Russ asked, "What do you think we should do for Black History month?" It popped into my head that maybe when we had those after-lunch school sings, we could sing the Black national anthem ["Lift Every Voice to Sing"]. Russ didn't know what it was, or maybe he knew what it was but he just wanted to hear us sing it, so I started singing it, and he said, "That was incredible. I never knew that you could sing." I didn't know. "You have to sing," he said. "I have to take you over to Barry [Soloway, the music teacher]."

Barry told me that Russ wanted me to sing it for him. I was really self-conscious about this, and I didn't want to do it, but I sung it and Barry said, "You have a very beautiful voice. Maybe we can work with something." After that, every time we had a school event, I sang. Then I thought, "Hey, I'm finally good at something on my own. It's not something Tina and I are doing together, it's just me." So that really gave me self-confidence. I had something that I was good at besides reading a book. So I started singing better and getting into acting. It made me want to read different types of things. It changed my whole outlook on everything.

Before that, most of what I read was only fictional things, like Judy Blume books. Then I started becoming interested in history, poetry by different authors, mostly Afro-American stuff. Russ had given me an album by a singer. It was Afro-American related and it got me interested in a whole lot of other things. Every time we wanted to know about something, Russ or Alice would bring in a book that had it there. It broadened our horizons a little bit. Everything wasn't a fiction book that had a happy ending.

Graduates often told me anecdotes about moments when they suddenly mastered a skill, or conquered a barrier, or developed a case of curiosity. Follow-up questions prompted descriptions about how students, with the help of their teachers, used these moments to forge pathways that led to sustained academic learning. Russ's accidental discovery of Kathy's musical talent, for example, tapped previously unknown interests and talents. This discovery then opened doors to African American music, poetry, and history, with Russ providing encouragement and curriculum material along the way.

When I read through all 40 interviews, I did not find any stories just like Kathy's. Instead, the graduates' stories were wonderfully varied. While taking care of animals was very important to Matthew Wilson,

Tosha Prince was more interested in starring in theatrical productions. Doodling on the computer led to an interest in computer graphic applications for Alec Cartwright, while his sister Jeanetta's experience modeling ancient Egyptian costumes grew into a love of fashion design. Each graduate's story was different; each had found a pathway to academic progress.

CPE's unique organization of the three central elements of its program—the curriculum, the role of students, and the role of teachers—enabled students to chart their own pathways. Using the graduates' words wherever possible, I will describe how these reforms promoted student success.

But not everyone agreed that CPE's program was effective. This chapter also gives dissident graduates and parents a chance to present their side of the story.

AN INTEGRATED AND THEMATIC CURRICULUM

Classroom activity centered not around the mastery of skills, nor around textbooks, but around themes organized by the teachers. Although these themes varied widely, all were broad enough to engage students in a variety of activities and to encourage them to develop multiple skills.

How teachers introduced these themes into the classroom can be seen in excerpts from the February 1993 letter Alice Seletsky wrote to parents of the children in her class.

> We've investigated a broad range of curriculum topics this year. Some of them emerged, as they often do, from the particular interests of an individual child or group; others were based on my own ideas of what is challenging, interesting, or necessary for the children to learn.
>
> Boats, sailing, and navigation were the themes early in the year. Children made models of ancient sailing ships, and engaged in experiments which involved navigational instruments, boat design, buoyancy. In October, we were asked to test a science/math computer game which is being developed at the Bank Street School. It fit in neatly with the other work that was going on. The game requires that teams of players, using information provided by the computer, find a fishing trawler lost at sea. Many skills are involved in playing the game: reading maps and the directional compass, charting a navigational course using coordinates, and solving mathematical problems involving speed and distance.

Our "official" social studies curriculum, which began in November, was a study of the lands of the ancient Middle East. We had group discussions about families and origins, how early people changed from nomadic hunters into farmers living in settled communities. Again, there was lots of model-making, map study, murals, pottery, and weaving, as well as the writing of individual research reports. We read Babylonian myths, discussed polytheism and monotheism, and explored the ways in which governments and laws came into being. We speculated on what daily life might have been for these early people. We also did a brief study of the Jews and read some parts of the Old Testament. We had a very interesting visit to the Jewish Museum and learned about archaeology and ancient artifacts. Currently, a group of children is working on an original dramatization of the story of Joseph and his brothers.

Choosing Activities

Students learned to choose among the myriad activities teachers organized for each curriculum theme—a practice that contrasts starkly with most American classrooms, where teachers drill students on discrete, sequential skills that educators have decided all students need to learn at the same time. At CPE, themes typically involved a field trip, perhaps to the Metropolitan Museum of Art, or Central Park, or the nearby Jewish Museum, or perhaps further afield, to Plymouth Plantation, or the District of Columbia. Students might read common material assembled by teachers, but they were always encouraged to branch out on their own. During their daily hour of "project time," students made individual choices, deciding if they wanted to write a play or a puppet show, to make a model, to create a piece of art related to the common theme, and so on.

When Leslie Stein's class studied ancient Egypt, for example, Heather Bush remembers, "Delaila and I made a King Tut death mask. It was a papier mache thing we painted all up. I was most impressed by it." For Jeanetta Cartwright, the same curriculum unit yielded different results: "We made a newspaper, the *Tut Times*. We made our own hieroglyphics and wrote to each other using those."

Student choice was not only a characteristic of each curriculum theme, it was a central feature of CPE's educational practice. Barbara Martinez, who came to CPE from a regular elementary school when her mother moved to East Harlem from the Bronx, found the contrast between the skill-oriented reading program at her former school and CPE's meaning-oriented approach to reading to be intensely liberating.

When I first came to CPE, I was really scared of having to see the same kind of packaged manipulative cards I'd had at my other school. I was so frightened of that. But it wasn't like that. I got to read books about people from other cultures. . . . It was such a great thing to read those "Monster" books.

Developing Habits of Mind

CPE's curriculum was organized not to "cover" particular information or to teach isolated skills, but rather to challenge students to think for themselves. Jimmy O'Rourke remembers:

We took a couple of field trips to Central Park. Some people did reports on the skating rink or the dairy. We made this game. We made a scale model of the park. I still have it. We put little dots on it. We had to answer questions about the park. If you got the answer right, you'd move a space. It was a neat little game. It was fun to make. We had papier mache for the castle and we painted it. There were little trees.

We had to come up with good questions. You didn't even think about the research. You're sitting there, looking through book after book, looking for something to use. It wasn't a strained process; it was more like a means to an end, and the end was fun, so the means became fun too.

Over time, students developed such habits of mind as asking questions, searching for and evaluating evidence, and developing and expressing their own opinions. Anessa Boland, who graduated from CPE in 1981, says her teachers Carol Mulligan and Bruce Kanze both used to turn her questions back to her in an effort to help her delve deeper.

When I asked a question, Carol would say, "That's an interesting question. Go look it up. If you have difficulty, I'll help you." Bruce would look at me funny and say, "I don't know. Let's go find out." That was something I really liked about Bruce. He really helped me.

Exploring Cultures

Most curriculum units involved exploring diverse cultures, past and present, through hands-on activities as well as reading and writing. Johnetta Baker says that what I enjoyed about the school was that you'd take a topic and go over it thoroughly, spend at least a month on it. We were doing Greek mythology. We did a play; we learned about Greek dress; we made Greek costumes; and we did a Greek feast. We learned all about the food they ate. I came to appreciate different types of mythology—African mythology, Greek mythology—and did a lot of reading on that.

Heather Bush believes that hands-on projects helped students make sense of foreign cultures.

We must have been talking about the Koran. We made a little mosque. . . . I think it puts you more in touch with what really happened. True, my mosque was 6 inches tall, but the thought that something like this was actually built full-scale, brick by brick, and the artwork on it was done by these wonderful artists. . . . I'm more of a book person now, but to create things with your hands and be proud of them when you're a kid is a big thing; it gives you confidence in your own interpretation of things.

For Jimmy O'Rourke, the class trip was the key to his making sense of the Pilgrims' culture.

That theme was a lot of fun, especially because you're here in New York City, in this big capitalist industrial society, and you're trying to learn about a time when there wasn't any of that. Growing up in the city your whole life, for a lot of kids, you just couldn't really place it because you had no real background to understand what that was all about.

Then, the class took a trip to Plymouth Plantation, where you're in the 1600s. You feel, "Ah ha." It clicks. You think, "Wait a minute, so this is what they had to deal with." Everyone got the biggest kick out of walking by a man working on a thatched roof. You were asking him what time it was. He'd look up to the sun, and he'd tell you. You'd look at your watch and say, "How do you do that?" Everyone was just amazed.

In general, CPE's holistic approach to the study of foreign cultures and past civilizations enabled students to achieve a multilayered understanding of the varieties of human social and cultural life, and gave them an appreciation of the complexity of historical development. Barbara Martinez pointed to how her study of ancient Troy spurred an interest in history.

For me it was a burning issue to learn about Troy. I wanted to know if it was real. I'd been reading so many books about Troy; some said it was a myth, and then others said it was a real city. The books were definitely a lot more sophisticated than I had known. I had the answers to what Troy was, but I couldn't stop. I felt this obsession: I had to learn everything about Troy.

For Tosha Prince, it was during the study of Greek mythology that she learned how to plunge deeply into another world.

I built a Greek arena with a theater. I made little people and I made costumes and I did this research project. I was only 10 years old. I did a project like that in college last year. Those are subjects that I didn't even study in junior high and high school, not until college.

Heather Bush made perhaps the largest claim about how CPE's curriculum units shaped the way she views the world.

I think the more you know, the less you feel you know, and you want to know more. When I got to junior high school, and high school, I felt that I had an understanding of a lot of things that other kids hadn't really experienced. At CPE, we did get to go to museums and we did get to talk about different cultures. It wasn't, "We have 2 weeks to talk about this right now, and you can't ask questions, because we don't have time for them." We live in a pretty small world these days, and it's important to know about other people.

Working Together

CPE curriculum units not only challenged students to think critically, and to become aware of the varieties of culture; they also taught students how to work collaboratively, especially during project time. Usually, two students worked together, as when Steve Hernandez joined with Spencer Calvin to build a ship. "Spencer started a ship with an actual frame. I wanted to join him because it was coming out so nicely, and he let me be a part of that." Similarly, Jeanetta Cartwright and Melissa Mata made a film. "I was friends with Melissa. In Alice's class, we made an animated film together. Alice had a movie camera. You move it and take a picture and move it. We had to cut out a lot of pictures from magazines and we moved things around."

Once students developed the habit of working together during project time, collaboration became a central feature of many activities—from ad hoc newspapers, to puppet shows, plays, bake sales, and mural painting. Kathy Title, one of "the Two Musketeers," along with Tina Pittman, conveys a sense of how far students could go on their own once they learned how to work together effectively.

> I'd go to Alice and say, "Alice, Tina and I have an idea. We want to do a puppet show, so what do we do?" Alice would say, "Write whatever you want the show to be about." We wanted to do *Winnie the Pooh*. We wrote a script. It was taken from one of the books but we had to get it together. Now what did we do? What do you need for a puppet show? You have to make puppets. We were allowed to sit there and make puppets—sew the clothing, paint and stuff the puppets. Then we need a stage. We were allowed to go in the empty room between Alice's class and Connie's class. It was a wood shop. We went back there and we planned our stage. We made our stage and we painted it. You did everything yourself. After it was completed, you were allowed to do the play for the class. We had the music all planned out. We had cues. When we put this on, it was so much fun. It seemed like a lot of work, but it was something we wanted to do and we did.

Of course, when students took on so much responsibility, their projects did not always work out as well as they did for Kathy and Tina. Sabelle Cooper remembers a flop.

> One time, Anessa Boland and I did a play, *Cinderella*. We were going to do a modern-day version. We wrote it and everything. We got these kids from another class to be in the play. It was so much responsibility. It was a big flop, and it was really disappointing, but I remember we worked really hard on it.

Two-person teams may have acted independently, but the rest of the class was always involved as well. Each team reported on its activities to the class, giving everyone an opportunity to share with and to learn from one other. Barbara Martinez observed this collaborative learning when she returned to CPE to do student teaching with Bruce. "I could ask any kid in the class what somebody else was doing, and they knew what they were studying; they knew why it was important; they knew where it fit in the larger scope of their study."

Collaboration had a number of benefits. First, it enabled students with little experience or few skills in one kind of activity to learn from more experienced or skillful classmates. It also enabled students to see that many different approaches were possible to a single problem. Jimmy O'Rourke remembers that when he worked on a project about cities, he discovered that Daniel Lopez's approach was more interesting.

> Daniel got really intricate in this one. I tried to help him and he got mad at me because I didn't have the patience for it. He was building this supermarket where you could take the roof off. He was making aisles and putting things on the shelves. He had to make little ice cream boxes, little cereal boxes, and stacking them to make it so realistic. I was saying, "Daniel, you can't do this. Draw them on." And he said, "No, we have to do it this way." His was 10 times better than ours.

Jasmine Stevens credits her fellow classmates with teaching her how to use the computer: "I met students who taught me something new. Johnny Stein and Mark were so smart. . . . We had a computer in our classroom and they taught me how to use it. When I couldn't get it from anybody else, they sat down and taught me how."

For Anessa Boland, playing the teacher role left an impression.

> In Carol Mulligan's class, there was a little girl who had a hard time. She was dyslexic or she had some other learning disability. . . . We used to have quiet reading time and she would try to get past one page. If she couldn't make it to the end of the page, she would go to the bathroom and cry. So I started reading with her. She used to ask me, "What's this word? What does this word mean?" If I knew, I would tell her, but then we would go and ask Carol Mulligan together.

Collaboration also helped students to develop confidence in their ability to work without adult supervision. When Jeanetta Cartwright and Melissa Mata made their animated film, "it was good because it was just me and her working on it. . . . Alice wasn't supervising. It gave us a sense of independence. We got a chance to explore our own ideas." Furthermore, collaboration introduced children to the challenges of working with others, Jeanetta adds, "If I wanted to do something and she didn't want to do it, we had to compromise."

Critiques of progressive education often charge schools like CPE with having a free-for-all curriculum. The testimonies of CPE graduates, however, suggest otherwise. By drawing on their own interests, teachers were able to design themes broad enough to cover a variety of disciplines. As a result, students not only learned specifics about a certain theme, but simultaneously were encouraged to think critically, to make their own choices, to learn about diverse cultures, and to collaborate with others.

MAKING AND EXPRESSING MEANING THROUGH ART

While CPE's curriculum necessitated that students create meaning from possibilities that teachers proposed, integrating the arts into those curriculum themes provided the means to do so. Art, writing, drama, and music became primary vehicles for students to express their ideas, feelings, and fantasies to others. Graduates were so adamant about the importance of each art form that each is examined individually in the following sections.

The Visual Arts

Most elementary schools integrate art into the curriculum by having students cut out and color turkeys at Thanksgiving, draw ships for Columbus Day, and so on. But at Central Park East, art was more than an activity, it was a valued means of expression.

Trips to nearby art museums—the Metropolitan Museum of Art, the Guggenheim, the Jewish Museum, and the Whitney—gave students chances to see and experience works of art exhibited for the public. These trips reinforced teachers' classroom lessons about the importance of art as a form of communication.

Drawing from their museum experiences, students customarily shared the art objects they created during project time with the class and later exhibited them school-wide. As students gained a sense that their work was worth showing to others, they gained pride in themselves. That kind of pride is clear in Marlo Jones's words, as she remembers one of her creations: "I made a cobra, and, my God, how I wish I still had that thing."

Natasha Blake recalls two projects she made with particular satisfaction—a robot and a kite.

> I used a battery, and his eyes were spinning. Then I made this beautiful hawk kite. You know Eyeore's bookstore? [children's bookstore that used to be on the Upper West Side]. Leslie was friends with a guy who worked there. He put my robot and my kite in the window to get people to come in.

Natasha's mother remembers just as vividly.

The arts and crafts were set up where they made the kids feel good about what they were doing. All the kites . . . were put on display. Natasha's was displayed downtown. Everything they did, they really wanted to do well, because that's how the teachers in that school made you feel.

While the visual arts began as only one part of each curriculum unit, a turn of fate made them a central part of the school's identity. In Alice Seletsky's fifth/sixth-grade class in 1982–83, several students were not engaging with her curriculum theme. They weren't reading much, they weren't doing interesting projects, and they seemed relentlessly bored and resistant, Alice remembers. At her urging, CPE hired Jane Andrias, who had experience as an open classroom teacher, to work part time with some of the students in Alice's class. In a previously empty room, Jane began teaching several students to draw and paint. She also went into Alice's classroom to give support and attention to students who asked for help. Soon, there was a group of students working intensively with Jane, some of whom were among those Alice had been worrying about, while others simply wanted to explore painting and drawing. Valerie Sanchez was one of the latter.

We drew in charcoal. We did a lot of still lives. [Jane] would set something on the table and we would draw it. I used to like that a lot. I was always praised for my artwork.

Jane worked at CPE for 2 years, gradually increasing her hours and the number of teachers with whom she worked. Then she went to Dalton, a nearby private school, to learn more about teaching art. After 2 years, Jane returned to CPE full time, to develop an art program. She later became CPE's Director.

At least five of the graduates I interviewed are pursuing careers in the arts. Among them is Daniel Lopez.

I was always making buildings or cars. . . . I remember drawing a lot. That's why my interest now is in art, because I did a lot of my drawings when I was a kid at CPE. . . . A lot of my creative talents I owe to CPE, because if I didn't have [a] project or that extra time to draw, maybe I would not have decided to go into art. I probably wouldn't have got into [the High School of] Art and Design or Buffalo State [College]. I could have been in accounting. . . . Creative wise, CPE inspired me.

Writing

As with art, CPE students and teachers did not approach writing as the mastery of mechanical skills, but as a means of expression. In a 1983 letter to parents, Alice Seletsky stressed the importance of writing in her classroom.

> Writing is an activity to which I give high priority. This year, I've been giving special attention to teaching children some techniques for revising and editing their work. It's a difficult thing for most of them to learn, and while we've made a good beginning, it's the kind of skill that develops with time, practice, and patience. I've included a sample of each child's work, which indicates the kind of writing he/she can do, and how each one goes about the business of editing, proofreading, rewriting.

Students' writing did improve "with time, practice, and patience" through daily journal writing. Teachers read journal entries regularly and wrote comments about them—unless children wanted their entries to remain private. A rich world of thought and feeling unfolded in these pages. Students wrote fanciful stories, discussed personal problems, and carried on dialogues with their teachers, sometimes on topics they were afraid to talk about out loud.

Cheryl DeSilver's journal helped her to overcome her dislike of writing and to face some personal concerns as well.

> I was making up stories about kids my age or younger. It wasn't my life through these people. It seemed to be somebody I wished I was. I remember one character; she had all these friends. I had some friends but I didn't have a gang, a herd of friends. I would write about these girls who were my age and who did things that I like to do but they had these personalities that were opposite of me.

In order to emphasize the value of students' written expressions, Alice Seletsky typed up the students' stories so they could create "books." Marlo Jones was one of the most-read story writers of the class of 1979.

> I got a chance to write stories, which were always shown around. When I would write a story, the teacher would read it to the class, too. They were mostly fantasy stories about children: I didn't go beyond my scope then. One was called *Crazy Town*. It was one of those stories where everything is backwards from regular. Another one was about a girl. There was a door in her basement, a door that she could go

through into another land. When I was at CPE, I was really happy about my writing, because everybody made such a big deal about it.

But some writing was about subject matter too private to share, Barbara Martinez remembers.

I had more of an opportunity to write my creative journal, to talk about who I was, or to duplicate the stories that I had heard that were important. That became a really good way for me to talk about things, even if I wasn't talking about them all the time at school.
    I did most of the writing in school, because we weren't very well off financially, so at home I didn't feel like I had much privacy. At home I didn't feel like I could commit anything to paper that could be read by someone. But writing was always private at school. At school, you could publish your little books, but it was something that you chose to do. If you did not publish them, that was fine too.

For Marla Baker, the journals became a vehicle for exploring emotional conflicts privately: "You could fold the page down and say, 'Carol, don't read this,' and she wouldn't read it. So she said. I don't think she did. We trusted her."
    Twelve students mentioned writing as an interest that they pursued in junior high and high school. Pia Gomez, whose poetry used to delight Alice Seletsky, continued writing throughout secondary school and was editor of her high school yearbook. When Marla Baker went from an East Harlem junior high school to one of New York's prestigious private high schools, writing remained her main academic interest. "When I got to Columbia Prep, I wrote a lot. I was on the literary magazine; eventually I was co-editor."
    A few students reported that daily writing had become a part of their lives, not only in school, but at home. Valerie Sanchez, said, "On my own, here in my house, I continued writing." In the same vein, Stephanie Gonzalez, who has not gone to college, reports:

To this day, I love to write. I think it has a lot to do with those journals. Journal time was my favorite. To tell you the truth, I was thinking about getting a diary at the end of the year. I said to myself, "I want to get myself a black and white book."

Drama

Drama was another important vehicle through which students explored meaning and learned to communicate it. Almost every student participated in a dramatic production. Student involvement in drama began in the early grades, when they not only played with puppets, but also wrote, produced, and directed their own puppet shows. By the time they were in fifth grade, these productions were elaborate.

Alice's classes' productions of Shakespearean dramas and Gilbert and Sullivan operettas figure prominently in graduates' memories. With so much work to do, and a variety of tasks to complete, there was room for everyone to make a contribution. Carmen San Jose was involved in the production end of things. "We used to make the frame from wood, and put the paint down. It was a good play because the scenery we did looked real. I was always willing to help out and paint." Stephanie Gonzalez was in Bruce's class, but she participated in Alice's class productions anyway: "We had to paint the murals for her, so we all got to know each other." Jeanetta Cartwright chose to work on a different part of the production: "We were in charge of making our own costumes. I think that had a lot to do with me going into fashion."

Other students participated as actors. Tosha Prince's stardom was born on Central Park East's stage. "I was in all the plays. I was always the leading lady. I was in *Julius Caesar* and I was Lady Macbeth. I was good. I got the drama award. Alice always knew I was going to go to Performing Arts High School, and I did."

Not everyone was enthusiastic about acting, however. Four graduates, Valerie Sanchez, Daniel Lopez, Carmen San Jose, and Steve Hernandez, all said they were too shy to perform before other people. Steve recalls:

> When I was in the fifth grade, they were doing a play and somebody was absent so I took his place for that day. It felt good. When I did that small scene, Alice asked, "That was good Steve, why didn't you take part?" I answered, "I'm not interested." I was very shy. I was intimidated that I might get laughed at.

Mastering Shakespearean English inhibited Greg Powers: "The different English—it was hard. The plays were hard to read." But other students enjoyed perfecting a difficult and beautiful language. According to Terry Britain:

> A lot of people were surprised we were able to handle Shakespeare. Basically, our teacher said, "Look, it's a little difficult, but it's not impossible," and it wasn't. Because it was presented to us in that manner, learning about Shakespeare and about the period and the country in which he wrote, it didn't seem so difficult. Of course, you have people saying, "Shakespeare can't be done by kids so young," but we did it and we knew the general concepts.

In Alvin Ortiz's description of the rehearsal of Alice's class plays, we can detect both pain and a sense of triumph.

> We used to fear the plays because Alice was a tough director. She wanted everything perfect. She used to tell us, "Work at it at home," and we would come in and [if] we weren't working on it she could tell right away. She would insist that we do it all correctly and she would work with you until you got it, in front of everybody. It helped; most of us were more outspoken by the time we graduated. There was no one who was shy within the group.

After he played Hamlet, Terry Britain grew to love the theater. At first, the theater projects "didn't seem like such a big deal." But then:

> My good buddy Eugene Davidson and I shared the role of Hamlet, each taking half. It was great. We did help each other as far as the character of Hamlet. There was one particular scene where Hamlet is talking to Ophelia, "Get thee to a nunnery." And he's supposed to be kind of losing it mentally. I was playing the role a little too straight and Eugene helped me with that. There was one time when he played that scene and he was really crazy. We were really close, but you had the little bit of competition. So we were both pushing each other. We both wanted to be the better Hamlet. We worked together. It was fun.

Music

CPE's music program was launched in 1978 as part of Deborah Meier's attempt to give the teaching staff a simultaneous preparation period. She hired Barry Soloway to lead daily all-school sings after lunch hour. Over time, Soloway began giving recorder lessons, and he organized a chorus and a rhythm orchestra for older children.

Barry came to CPE after an unhappy experience at a junior high school in Brooklyn: "I wanted to teach music heart to heart, but I couldn't do it in double classes where the students were not quiet, paid no attention, and had no desire to learn music." At CPE, though, class could be a private lesson with one difficult child.

> In my third or fourth year at CPE, I taught one child an aria from *The Magic Flute*. I gave drum lessons to another troubled child. You can teach a lot through music. Care, discipline, concentration, emotional power. You can heal yourself through music.

Through music some students gained confidence that they were good at something. As they learned the discipline of concentrated practice, as they mastered their songs and performed in public, students' sense of competence, and their confidence in their ability to learn, grew much stronger. Jasmine Stevens articulates well how Barry helped her grow.

> Barry helped me a lot with music. . . . In Alice's class, we did *HMS Pinafore*. You had to audition. I auditioned for Buttercup. [After I was chosen,] I had to sing this song. Oh God, it was so funny. We had to make our own costumes and find things from home and get made up together. Barry played the music and suggested how we should sing. You felt so professional because the stage was so large. The whole class was in it. That was the first and probably the last time I heard about Gilbert and Sullivan.
>   We were going to have an assembly where you could do any talent you wanted. I wanted to sing, "Send in the Clowns," because it was my favorite song. It still is. He got the music for me. Every day, I would come to him and he would spend so much time on it. He never said, "I only have a half hour. . . ." He went over my song with me and we found the right key. He gave me enough courage to sing it in front of the whole school. I was terrified, so he used to make jokes about the crowd. "Just picture them not even paying attention to you." He gave me that encouragement to do it.

Marie Spain thought Barry Soloway and the music program was "the best thing in the world [that] I got from CPE. . . . I always remember having a good time at CPE. . . . I always had a very strong desire to learn as much as I could because it was fun and important. [At other schools] some kids don't feel that way and they drop out."

Not all students loved the music program. Indeed, there were students who resisted Barry's repeated calls for concentration, discipline, and quiet. Tosha Prince, who became a soloist at CPE performances, remembers Barry as "a real pain. He wanted our complete attention, and at that age, it's hard to give it. So he would separate you from your friends."

Marlo Jones described her resistance to Barry's demands. "I gave the teacher a hard time back then. It didn't happen often really, but me and a couple of kids, we delayed on purpose, trying to skip out of chorus if possible."

Despite such resistance, 19 graduates from CPE I and three from CPE II reported that the interest in music they developed at CPE continued in junior and senior high school, making music the interest most followed up in secondary school. Looking back, Natasha Blake says her music education at CPE shaped the kind of learner she became, indeed, shaped the kind of human being she became. "I don't think I would be the way I am if I hadn't gone to CPE. I'm into everything, into every kind of music. I have all kinds of friends. I'm broad-minded." Natasha has continued singing. Today she's writing and recording songs. "Now I'm doing love songs, about a boy and a girl. They really like each other. They get together, but I don't say it that way. I use dancing as the image. I'm using the dancing as a kind of communicating between the guy and the girl."

CPE's emphasis on the creative arts as a vehicle for the expression of personal feeling and meaning encouraged many graduates to value artistic expression in their later lives. In part, this was a matter of participation; many of those who completed CPE went on to East Harlem Performing Arts and Harbor Academy for Performing Arts, where they continued to develop talents and interests in instrumental music, drama, dance, or singing that they'd discovered at CPE.

But it also appears to be something more, a continuing interest in and openness to artistic expression that some graduates say might not have existed had they attended a different elementary school. Terry Britain sells clothing on Manhattan sidewalks to put himself through Baruch College of the City University of New York as a business major. He says CPE's drama productions and art projects shaped his personality, by making him more open to artistic expression and artistic people.

> I really like live theater and usually get to see one or two shows a year. Every time I go and see one, I think, "Oh, I should do this more often," because there's a great feeling from live theater and it's better than sitting around watching TV. If I hadn't gone to CPE, I would never have seen it, or maybe I would have thought of it as sissy stuff. But at that time I was still young enough. And I saw people like me doing it so it didn't seem so bad. The artistic projects helped to open me up to more artistic people and to become more rounded.

He doubts he'd be paying for his college education by doing street theater to sell merchandise ("talking boxer shorts") if he hadn't attended CPE.

GUIDING AND ENCOURAGING STUDENTS

Creating integrated curriculum units and helping students make and communicate meaning through the arts required CPE teachers to redefine their role. Rather than serving as judges of performance and sources of knowledge, teachers supported student exploration, acting as guides to new realms of experience and encouraging the development of strengths.

Encouragement and Competition

Instead of grading students, teachers provided encouragement. They constantly observed what students were doing, made suggestions, and pointed out areas that could be developed further. The teachers' confidence in their students and their high expectations provided an important motivation to excel, Jasmine Stevens believes.

> I don't think they gave rewards for doing something. It was considered your duty; you were supposed to get good grades. If you got a 90, that's what you're supposed to get. It wasn't like, "Someone got a 90; everyone clap for that person." It was nothing like that. You didn't get rewarded because it was just supposed to happen.

When a student had problems learning something, the teacher tried to offer help without damaging the student's confidence. Terry Britain offers an example from his first project at CPE.

> I did a report on space. I was 8 years old. I went home and pretty much copied paragraphs out of Funk and Wagnall's encyclopedia. At that school, they were always encouraging. They would never come out and say, "This is terrible; I'm disappointed." In this case, Connie said something about it wasn't very original or imaginative. At the time, I felt, "Hm, I have a little work to do." It was a challenge to think about what I could do better next time.

While Terry Britain's testimony refers to his initial encounter with CPE, Valerie Sanchez's comments about her relationship with Alice Seletsky give a sense of how CPE teachers provided criticism and encouragement to their students over time.

> Alice is a tremendous teacher. I was in the fifth grade. I hadn't learned well my multiplication tables yet, and I was embarrassed about that; I hadn't mentioned it yet. At one point, Alice realized it. I was expecting insults but she sat me down, she gave me a math book to help me in that area. I learned the multiplication tables and then I kept on with the rest of the book; that was it.
>   Alice always encouraged me to do my best. One time I did a project, I don't know on what, and she wasn't very satisfied with it.

It seemed I didn't put my best into it; maybe I got lazy then. Her way of telling me was—calmly, she told me that she didn't think I had put enough time and effort into it, that I could have done better. She was accepting the project, just the next time, to try harder because she knew what my potentials were, what I was able to do.

I remember her always being helpful. When she saw that I was doing something that was good, she always encouraged it. She would bring out some errors in my writing. I never had problems accepting her corrections and changing them. Alice liked me. I wasn't a bad student; I tried to do my best. I was always me. That confidence she had in telling me what was wrong, what could have been done a certain way, helped me.

The teachers' supportiveness freed students of anxiety and therefore opened them to exploring what they did not know. For Barbara Martinez, who had a brother close to her age, with whom she had always been compared, this was especially important.

I felt really peaceful in Debbie's classroom. I definitely knew I wasn't going to be compared to anyone else. It happens with siblings relatively close in age. I was a shy child. I wasn't comfortable being judged by a piece of paper. I never felt like I could enjoy someone looking at me and saying, "Oh, this is excellent work," when it wasn't excellent work, it was just me doing whatever it was I had to do so that I wouldn't get attention.

I don't think I was shy in [Debbie's] classroom. I definitely felt more accepted, and didn't feel as intimidated. That was good for me; I enjoyed that. I could walk in every day and not worry about people, not worry about a test, not worry about how many stars [I would get for my work], almost like I was my own star.

Barbara believes this approach has lasted and helped her succeed at Brown University.

I don't compete. I don't say competition is bad, but my goal in life is not to go out and have more than that person has. I want to have what I want. I want to be able to say what it is that I want, not compared to the guy next door. I have a lot more power when I know exactly what I need. I can ask myself the questions and see where it is that I want to go. I don't ever have to say, "This person is the standard."

Even though teachers de-emphasized competition, peer pressure among students did propel some students to strive to stand out. According to Jasmine Stevens:

> Competition was definitely there with some students, but it wasn't encouraged by the teachers. You never heard the teacher mention anything like that. It came about by having a friend. If your friend got one grade and you got another, the next time you tried even harder to get it.

Because teachers were supportive and encouraging of everyone, the students' competition did not create the kind of destructive anxiety that may deter a child from taking risks. Jasmine Stevens argues:

> It wasn't a pressure situation, because you weren't going to lose if you didn't get it. I never talked about it. Me and my friends never sat down and said, "I'm going to get a higher grade than you." It was never like that. Everyone competed within themselves. I never said, "How come I didn't get that?" to someone. I just said in my head, "Next time, you're going to do better than that person."

Freedom from competitive activity made sharing and collaboration possible, Jasmine concludes.

> There was one minuet I couldn't get [on the violin]. There was a lot of note changing. [The other children] taught me that. Because it was such a warm atmosphere, it felt like it was natural to help one another, to teach each other things.

Mrs. Wilson adds that when her son Matthew was having trouble learning to spell, another student helped him get over the hump.

> Matthew didn't feel funny or strange. The kids did their work together in groups of three or four. He had one kid in particular who helped him spell. He was a wonderful kid a couple of years older than Matthew.

Guidance

By developing practices that provided each individual child with advice, corrections, and encouragement, CPE faculty guided a student toward solving a learning problem particular to that child or toward moving on to new levels of understanding. For example, when citywide reading test results indicated that Natasha Blake was below a second-grade reading level, her mother asked Carol Mulligan, Natasha's teacher, what could be done. Natasha remembers:

> Carol said, "Calm down, calm down." She didn't neglect any other of her kids, but during lunch time, or my playtime, she kept reading to me. And when I was home, my mother would read to me. After that happened, there was a library nearby that I used to go to get books. I just read and read. I had bookshelves full of books. Next thing I know, my reading level went up until it was two grades above.

Teachers continually worked to improve their ability to observe their students. One parent remembered a particular tool he found one teacher using on his first visit to CPE: "Lucy Matos . . . showed me that they had a learning chart for each child in that class. Each day, they marked down what the child had done and what they wanted that child to work on the next day."

At times, their drive to improve their own understanding of their students led CPE faculty outside the walls of their school. In 1975, CPE teachers teamed up with three researchers from the Educational Testing Service (ETS) to do an intensive study of how children learn to read. To analyze what children did—sound out words, guess word meanings, skip difficult words—teams consisting of one ETS staff member, one classroom teacher, and one observer interviewed teachers and children, gathered children's work samples and oral reading samples, measured their linguistic performance, and observed what they did in the classroom. The study concluded that while each child learns to read in a unique way, these individual paths could be categorized as three distinct styles of reading acquisition (Bussis, 1985). Working on this study not only helped CPE's staff to develop strategies for teaching reading that respected each child's learning style, but enabled the faculty to gain a sense of confidence in their expertise.

In addition to their collaboration with ETS, CPE teachers began working in 1978 with Patricia Carini at the Prospect Center, which had developed a program designed to help teachers observe and appreciate what students do.

During one summer she spent at Prospect, Alice Seletsky used the center's method to help her understand Matthew Wilson's problems with writing. Alice remembers feeling that Matthew was articulate in other ways while writing was a struggle; he couldn't spell, his handwriting was almost unreadable, he inverted word order, and so on. Alice didn't always push students with writing problems very hard, figuring they would find other ways of expressing themselves. In Matthew's case, though, she decided to see if she could help him. She went to the Prospect Summer Institute after Matthew's fifth-grade year ended, bringing his writings with her. As she read his work aloud to herself and others over and over, she gradually came to appreciate that Matthew was expressing intense feelings, complicated thoughts, and a lot of meaning despite his technical problems. As a result of the insights she gained at Prospect, Alice worked closely with Matthew in sixth grade, assuring him that she would help him with spelling as long as he made the effort to express his ideas as best he could. This bargain "freed Matthew, [and] made it more comfortable for him to express himself," Matthew's mother remembers. By the end of the year, he was writing longer stories and even won a commendation for working hard and making progress.

Mrs. Wilson points to how even the school's director took an active hand in regularly guiding the students.

> My daughter Julia [Matthew's older sister] had a very intimate experience with Debbie in her journal. Debbie would write regularly. No matter how busy Debbie was, she did keep tabs on all the kids through their journals. She wrote some of the most wonderful things in Julia's journal. Once, Julia was writing about her rabbit and Debbie homed right in on that. She would write, "Yes, I feel like that myself, but have you ever thought about this?" It was always a growth experience. She didn't write, "That's wonderful, dear." It wasn't patronizing at all; it was always quite magical, I felt, when I read those journals later.

As with writing, CPE's approach to reading offered an opportunity for teachers to respectfully guide their students. In February 1983, Alice Seletsky wrote to parents:

> Lots of reading goes on all day—children read aloud to each other, everyone reads at Quiet Reading Time. And I read aloud, at the end of the afternoon, while the children draw and sketch and listen. It's always a particularly nice time of day for me. This year we've read *Bridge to Terebithia*, *A Christmas Carol*, stories by I. B. Singer, Babylonian myths, and parts of the Old Testament. Our current book is *David and the Phoenix*.

Jasmine Stevens remembers that Alice read to the class just after snack time: "We used to sit. Everyone had a spot. She would read things that I probably wouldn't read on my own." Lola Johnson got so engrossed in the stories Alice read aloud that she dreaded missing a day of school: "Did they read more of the story?"

Reading aloud did more than introduce students to exciting stories that they would not have picked up on their own—it opened them up to the emotional impact of literature. Serving as a student teacher, 12 years after her graduation from CPE, Barbara Martinez describes one such moment teacher Bruce Kanze created.

> Once we had such a bad day with the kids. They were screaming; they were hitting each other; they were being very rotten, mean. . . . At the end of this terrible day, Bruce pulls out this book and starts reading to them. We've already had two talks about misbehavior. But this time, he says, "We're going to count this day as officially over. We are going to see if tomorrow we can have a better day, because I think we all had a pretty bad day." He reads from the poetry book for a while and then stops, saying, "Some of you guys might not like this because this is from a college English poetry book." And they said, "Read on, read on." It was beautiful poetry, love poems. By the time they left, everyone felt so much better.

During "quiet reading time," students could select whichever books they wanted to read on their own. Some students used this period to read their favorite book over and over again. When Jeanetta Cartwright first came to Vivian Wallace's class, she would read the book "about two mice before I read anything else. I always grabbed that book and I would read it. Then when I was satisfied that I had read the book enough times, I would read something else." Jimmy O'Rourke remembers that even in sixth grade, when there were some assigned books to read, students still "had freedom to read what they wanted to. I read Judy Blume five times in a row rather than something else." But teachers noted when a child was reading the same book or type of book beyond the point where learning was still going on. Then, a teacher might suggest another book.

It didn't always work. Sometimes students resisted their teachers' advice. Valerie Sanchez says she frustrated Alice no end because "I used to love reading this comic type of book. I also used to like reading Nancy Drew mysteries. Everything was fiction, really. Alice was always trying to get me to read nonfiction books" (see Alice's comments in Appendix B).

Johnny Stein was similarly impervious.

> I had favorite books, fantasy novels, that I would read again and again and again. Alice tried to get me to read Dickens. She said, "You are capable of reading stuff that's really great, so why don't

you give it a try?" I read maybe 100 pages of one Dickens novel and said, "No."

But over time, most students explored a variety of reading material. Alec Cartwright gives Bruce credit for helping him become a voracious reader. "He encouraged me a lot to read. By the time I was in fifth and sixth grade, I wasn't reading these regular picture books. I was reading novels." Bruce Kanze influenced Anessa Boland's reading habits as well.

He said, "Explore. Read. There are a whole lot of books. There are other authors. . . ." After I finished at CPE, I loved to read. I read anything I laid my hands on.

Evaluation

Another means of maximizing teacher support for student efforts was CPE's unique grading policy. Teachers did not assign students numerical or alphabetical grades for their performance of different tasks; instead, they met twice a year with each student and his or her parents. In addition, teachers wrote biannual letters to each student and his or her parents describing the student's progress. Almost always, the tone was warm and positive; the list of student accomplishments was long and detailed; the areas needing additional work were described in a way that made progress seem attainable. As an example, see Alice Seletsky's letter to the parents of Valerie Sanchez, in Appendix B. While some parents and students were uncomfortable with the lack of numerical guideposts, especially at first, most graduates echoed Terry Britain's endorsement of the school's nontraditional evaluations.

It wasn't that you felt uninformed about how you were doing, because they had teacher conferences and biannual reports on the progress of the students. They were personal so you got much more information. I knew, and my mom knew, exactly how I was doing, both my weaknesses and my strengths.

Building on Strengths

In-depth progress reports provided more than a means of motivating students to improve their skills in areas where they were weak. They helped encourage students to follow up their interests in order to develop areas of academic strength.

Teachers encouraged students who were having problems mastering a skill to find another activity that would engage their interest and help them to feel they were especially good at something; they could go back to overcome their weakness later, when they were ready. Again, Matthew Wilson provides an example. In first, second, and third grade, Matthew's teachers did not push him to read. "Debbie understood," Mrs. Wilson remembers. "She told me the best thing we could do for Matthew was to leave him alone." Matthew loved to play with animals and build things. He began reading later.

Another example of teachers designing activities specifically for students who were having trouble concerned Kareem Walton. Marla Baker tells the story.

> There was someone in my class, Kareem, who had a discipline problem. Bruce realized he was really interested in writing stories and working with children. Kareem wrote this play for children. Bruce would let us go every day to work on this play with these little kids. We performed it. Kareem was so happy. I remember thinking this would really help him. I remember him wanting authority all the time. Maybe it did help him because he got respect and authority from doing the play.

But it was not only students having academic problems who were encouraged to develop their own areas of academic strength and expertise. Believing that each child had unique interests, strengths, and ways of learning, CPE teachers tried to help every student gain mastery in self-chosen areas. According to the telephone survey, they succeeded—more than 90% of the 86 graduates surveyed reported that they had one or more strengths when they entered junior high. Slightly more than half reported having one strength, while more than four in ten said they had more than one. Only three students (less than 4%) reported having no strengths.

Another means of assessing whether CPE succeeded in helping students become strong learners through developing particular skills and interests is to ask another question: "Did you develop any interests in CPE that you continued in junior high school and high school?" Of the 74 graduates who responded, 63 answered "yes" (85%), and only 11 answered "no" (15%). The list of reported interests reflects the school's emphasis on the arts: music (22), art (17), reading (13), writing (12), and drama (10).

To describe how CPE helped students develop strengths that would endure and help them become successful learners, I present two of the 17 students who cited art as an interest. The stories of Alec and Jeanetta Cartwright, brother and sister, indicate that when teachers take students' interests seriously, students may develop passions in elementary school that not only will help them succeed in secondary school, but will carry through to adulthood.

When I asked Alec, home from New York State University at Albany, if he considered himself an artistic person, he made a connection to CPE without hesitation.

> That developed at CPE, when they first got the Texas Instrument computers over there. I can remember spending my recess time fiddling on the computer in Bruce's class. I could always play ball. I figured, since I have this interest, let me try it. I'd try to get this little extra time. I tried to do graphics, making things. I tried to use it as best as I could.
>
> I'm currently focusing on a degree in computer science. I want to do something in the computer field. I like computers, but not so much the technical part. I like computer animation, what you see on TV commercials. That's what I'm interested in. I could do something like that if I had the chance.

For Jeanetta, modeling the Nefertiti costume made by Leslie Stein's friend for the Metropolitan Museum of Art made a lasting imprint. Jeanetta's mother remembers that Mark Lutsky, an assistant principal, "always used to tell me I should enroll her in some kind of modeling school. I think it started from the ancient Egyptian costumes." Jeanetta's interest in fashion was reinforced by the work she did for a school play. "I remember doing a lot with the costumes when we performed a play in Alice's class. We were in charge of making our own costumes. I think that had a lot to do with me going into fashion." That interest continued to blossom at Brooklyn Tech High School. She later earned an associates degree in fashion buying and merchandising at FIT before joining her brother at Albany State to earn her BA degree. When she completes her college program,

> I want to go back to study display and exhibit, like window designing. That's something I just want to study for myself. I really don't want to pursue a career in that, because that's not an easy field to get into. I would like to be a buyer in a department store.

OPPOSING VIEWPOINTS

While most students were positive about the way CPE restructured the roles of teachers and students, reinvented the curriculum, and created comfortable classroom environments, several students dissented: Three students even said they would not send their child to a school like CPE.

Jill Hill was most negative about CPE. Jill belonged to one of the school's first graduating classes. Before she began junior high school, her family moved from New York; Jill and her younger sister Kim, who had attended CPE through fifth grade, then entered another big-city school system, where they had trouble. Placement tests administered by the new school system revealed serious academic deficiencies. Jill blamed CPE.

> If they said, "Open a book," you didn't really have to read it. You could open it and write notes to your friends, because they never asked you what was in the book after. They never questioned you about the book to help you remember detail or to make you understand if there was some sort of moral. What was the book about? How do you feel? I don't remember that. . . . At this age, you did everything to avoid doing anything. I don't think I read a book the entire time I was there.

Eventually Jill earned a Bachelor of Fine Arts degree. She is now working as a graphics designer. But she continues to feel handicapped by gaps in her education that she blames on CPE.

Terry Britain thinks CPE is "amazing, phenomenal," but believes it should adopt more traditional approaches to teaching "basic skills."

> Math is as pure a science as there is and you have to learn the basics. I don't think there is any alternative way of learning math. You can have games and everything but when it comes down to it, you have to know your times tables and you have to know how to do long division.

Sabelle Cooper, who recently graduated from Mount Holyoke, shared Terry's reservations.

> I had a decent experience at CPE. I think CPE is good in teaching values, teaching children sharing and expressing themselves in whatever mode. When I was there, it was a very ethnically mixed school, and I think that's important. It teaches good teacher–child relations, because the teachers aren't so way up here, the students way down here. And things like that are good. But I think for basic learning skills, something was lacking.

Dori Prince, who graduated from CPE II after attending primary grades in Jamaica, isn't sure CPE is the right school for everybody.

Some kids can't survive in such a free environment. If you sit there and take a nap, or you write notes to your friend for the entire reading period, you're not getting better in your reading.

CONCLUSION

While there were dissenters, most graduates described CPE classrooms as comfortable, inviting, and rich environments. The walls were covered with colorful objects: students' artwork, newspaper articles, time lines, and pictures related to curriculum themes. There were no rows of desks arrayed to face the teacher in the front of the room; instead, there was an area with a sink and a stove for cooking snacks, a loft for resting, a reading area with pillows on the floor, a math area with several desks clustered together. Some rooms housed animals—snakes, gerbils, frogs, or rabbits—while others had laboratory setups for science experiments.

Each classroom had its own book collection, stocked with a variety of books, on shelves low enough for children to browse through. Since each classroom contained students of two different grades, fifth and sixth, for example, or third and fourth, the books ranged in difficulty. They also spanned a range of interests, from Nancy Drew mysteries and cartoon versions of classics to Judy Blume novels about teenage life, classic plays and novels, and nonfiction as well.

Classrooms also contained a variety of materials for creating projects. During project time, which lasted at least an hour each day, students made models out of papier mache, or they brought in egg cartons from home to make buildings, and light bulbs to make maracas for the Puerto Rican Day parade. Jimmy O'Rourke's reaction to his kindergarten classroom captures the students' excitement: "The rooms were so much fun. It was like you wish your room could be that big at home, and have so many things to do."

Most graduates credited CPE, with these rich classroom environments, with enabling them to become successful students. Graduates identified three key areas where CPE's redefinition of educational practice contributed to their progress.

1. Classroom activity, centered around curriculum themes organized by the teachers, gave students the opportunity to explore and choose activities that engaged their interest, and stimulated the development of critical thinking skills.
2. Rather than serving as sources and purveyors of knowledge, teachers provided support, guidance, and encouragement to students.

3. The classrooms themselves facilitated exploration, active learning, and collaboration, rather than one-way communication from teachers to students.

These critical features of CPE practice were not rigidly spelled out when the school was established; rather, they evolved as the staff worked together to solve problems emerging in their classrooms and in the school as a whole. Yet while the schools' educational practices evolved, they rested on a set of underlying principles about the nature of teaching and learning, enunciated by Snyder, Lieberman, Macdonald, and Goodwin (1992) in a description of more recent Central Park East I classrooms.

1. Each individual has the drive and capability to make meaning of experience; and every individual is brilliant at some things.
2. Knowledge is not a thing or a set of behaviors that is passively received, but rather it is constructed by people motivated by "the human impulse to care, to seek worthwhile experience, and to making meaning of that experience" (p. 47).
3. The construction of knowledge takes place in social settings where people are accountable to and learn from others.

These principles of "progressive education" put the learner—not the teacher, or the school, or the curriculum—at the center of the educational experience.

But CPE graduates attribute their school success to more than the educational practices and principles spelled out in this chapter; just as crucial was the school's emphasis on nurturing the emotional and social development of each child. The next chapter will examine how the CPE schools carried out this task.

❧ 3 ❧

Pathways to Emotional and Social Growth

If you had any problems, you could go talk to Russ on a one-to-one basis, and he would ask us how do we feel about things. That was very helpful to me. When I didn't do well in a subject, or on my reading test, I would go to him and ask him why I didn't do well. He would tell me why and he helped me improve my study habits.

I was brought up with just my mother. I didn't really have a male at home that could give me the support that I needed. But at the school, I had a male role model that I could look to. He gave me support as if I was his child. I didn't have him for class, but he was always there for us.

He used to take eight of us, every other week in the summer, just to get together and talk about different things that were going on among us, helping us get some respect for ourselves, some dignity. He kept us together, kept us in line. . . .

At times, he would pull us out of class, one by one, and walk us around the block and just talk. It was sort of, "How have you been? How's everything at home? How's your mother? How's your brother?" That kind of support. That school really helped me, helped me a lot.

(Greg Powers)

MANY CPE GRADUATES identified CPE's contribution to their social and emotional growth as being even more important than its contribution to their academic progress. When 84 graduates were asked, "What were the most important things you gained from going to CPE?" 43 students chose "getting along with people," 27 "self-esteem," 23 "respect for others," 15 "know how to deal with authority/adults," and 7 "social concern." Altogether, graduates selected these social and emotional gains 115 times, while they selected academic gains only 77 times.

The students' responses are consistent with CPE's educational philosophy, which has deep roots in the progressive tradition. For nearly a century, progressive educators have argued that schools should foster not only academic learning, but also the development of morality, citizenship, emotional health, and social competence. The fact that CPE's staff share these values is inherent in the very design of this study. It was the teachers who suggested I include questions that asked students about their participation in activities outside of school, their values, their plans for the future, and the long-lasting impact of CPE on their personal growth in general.

"LIKE A FAMILY"

> If something was really bothering you, Alice was your mother; she was your big sister; she was your best friend. You could tell her anything. You have that at home, but then to have it at school too, it's like you're always home. It made life so much fun, it really did.
>
> (Kathy Title)

When students described their years at CPE, the phrase they used most often was that the school was "like a family." Dozens of students, each in their own way, said that the school was not an impersonal setting organized around rigid rules, nor was it a threatening place where they would be compared and judged. Rather, CPE was a warm, caring place, a place where students felt safe and protected, where they felt respected and valued and loved.

Classrooms Like Home

CPE's small size and the continuity of its classrooms combined to foster this warmth and intimacy. The school literally remained small enough so that everybody knew everybody. When CPE reached 250 students and 12 adults, the staff decided not to expand, even though there were dozens of parents clamoring to enroll their children. Instead, CPE established a second small school, which became CPE II. Later, River East was established.

CPE also kept students and their teachers together for 2 years, giving students a sense of continuity, and enabling teachers to get to know their students more deeply than would have been possible in 1 year.

At CPE, "family" meant more than a tight-knit classroom with continuity; the whole school was bound together with intimate ties. Members of the school community got to know each other by working together on school-wide projects like whole-school sings, opera and drama productions, camping trips, and fundraisers. Older children assisted teachers with younger children and participated in the setup and cleaning of the cafeteria after "family-style" lunches. And teachers got to know students who weren't in their classrooms, as they worked together making scenery for plays, practicing songs in the chorus, or preparing for athletic competitions.

Actual family relationships further reinforced CPE's intimacy and unity. Because CPE's admissions policy gave preference to siblings, many graduates had brothers or sisters in the school. Furthermore, since the children of CPE staff also had preference in admissions, many teachers had their own children attending the school. As the children of the staff became friends with other CPE students, the familial relationships between teachers and students thickened. "Russ was really friendly, and I liked his daughters," Jasmine Stevens remembers. "He was [an assistant] principal but he tried to mix with us. So he could understand how we acted towards him."

Jeanetta Cartwright says that her family became very close with several teachers at CPE.

> Vivian and Pam came and visited with us and went swimming with us in second grade. I was taking gymnastic lessons at the Y and Leslie came and watched me. And I remember in second grade, it was a big thing when Vivian was pregnant with Benjamin. The whole class was centered around her giving birth, because that was a big thing for us. . . . And before that, we went to Leslie's wedding. It was a Jewish wedding and the rabbi was saying that it was a blessing because there was so many children. . . . We were all very close.

CPE classrooms had a homey feel that reinforced the students' sense that they were with their families rather than in an impersonal institution. Some classrooms had area rugs and others had colorful pillows, so children could sit on the floor to listen to stories. Several teachers built lofts for children to rest or nap on.

On her first day at CPE, Valerie Sanchez was struck by the homey feel of Connie Brady's third/fourth-grade classroom.

> It wasn't the ordinary classroom with chairs all in a row. It looked so weird, like a big living room. . . . It had a kitchen, too. That really shocked me.

Animals, which children brought home over school breaks, became important links between home and school. Mrs. Wilson says that her son's love for classroom pets developed into a major part of her family tradition. "They were breeding tadpoles and frogs, so we had those frogs over a vacation. . . . It meant a lot to Matthew. He just loved them. He loved watching them." She also remembers when the class "went on a trip to Chinatown to buy the ingredients for soup. At the store, they had a big barrel of turtles to sell for soup. Matthew felt terrible that they were going to be sold for soup, so he bought a turtle and the turtle lived in our bathtub for about 18 months."

Classroom kitchen areas contributed to making the classroom an extension of the family home. Mrs. Blake says that when her daughter learned to cook at CPE, she brought her new skills home and shared them with her mother. "Natasha would come home from school, and say, 'We cooked asparagus in school today. Oh mommy, can we cook it at home?'"

CPE's concern with food was more than a matter of having children learn to cook snacks for each other; sharing nutritious food was one of the building blocks of the CPE family. The lunch hour was a time when CPE members could relax together without screaming, fighting, or food throwing.

After school, sharing food continued through potluck suppers. These communal rituals were not only important fund raisers, but a way for members of the school family to share cultural traditions. Vicki Pittman recounts: "Whenever I think of CPE, I think of Digna because I used to always tell her to make her Spanish dishes for me, and she would try to show me how to cook them."

Respect and Love

While CPE classrooms contributed to fostering a sense of family, more important was the way adults in school behaved toward children. According to the graduates, adults at CPE drew on their own parental feelings and experiences when they interacted with students, rather than being remote authority figures whose job it was to establish rules, set standards, and evaluate academic progress. Accordingly, they exuded warmth and caring in interpersonal interactions; they respected and paid attention to each individual child; and they concerned themselves with all of the child's needs—for friendship and good times, for good health and self-esteem, for autonomy and self-knowledge, for social competence and personal identity. Finally, like parents, they did not set boundaries on their caring; after school and outside the classroom, CPE teachers went far beyond the kind of help school personnel usually provide students.

When graduates talked about teachers, they almost always began with the fact that they called them Alice or Bruce, rather than Ms. Seletsky or Mr. Kanze—as if this symbolized the student–teacher relationship or perhaps even shaped the way children thought about school personnel. Marlo Jones was one of many graduates who said that using first names made a real difference.

We got to call [our principal] Debbie, and that never happened in any other school. You could think of your teachers as people, not just teachers. They were regular people. . . . It wasn't that strict teacher–student relationship.

Steve Hernandez adds that using first names helped create closeness not only between a student and his or her own teacher, but between all the teachers and students in the school.

It wasn't like "Professor" or "Teacher," or "Miss So-and-So." It was a first-name basis for everyone. That brought us close because they made us feel as if we were family with all the teachers. There was no exception. We all felt close.

Teachers infused their interactions with students with warmth and caring. "My teachers were my friends," Tosha Prince remembers. "They were my family. If you ever had a problem, they were there 100%. . . . That's just how loving they were." But, Tosha continues, that does not mean that teachers were soft or indulgent.

In sixth grade, it was day-to-day war with Alice Seletsky, but I always knew that she cared, I always did. She'd scream at me; sometimes, it seemed almost like she wanted to hit me. She never would, of course. And then the next minute, she'd have her arm around me, or she'd grab my hand. I had a really wonderful relationship with Alice. . . .
    When I had a problem, I would always have gone to Russ. He'd make everything better. I was Russ's pet, I know I was, and he was my favorite. I looked up to him, and whenever anything was wrong, Russ would come to me and just know things were wrong. He probably was a substitute father. He didn't spoil me or let me get away with anything; that's what was good about him. He was very real and very honest. If I was wrong, he would say, "Tosha, you're not being reasonable."

Kathy Title also remembers a special relationship with one of her teachers.

Alice was somebody you could tell everything to, even things that I wouldn't tell [my friend] Tina. Alice was one of those teachers that you only get once in a lifetime. You can't tell your mother everything; you can't tell your mother things you could tell your sister;

you can't tell your teacher things you would tell your mother; but
when you have that person all in one, you can tell them everything.
That's the type of person she was.

Adults at CPE gave each student individual attention. Valerie Sanchez
noticed that from her first day in Connie Brady's classroom.

Another thing that surprised me was the way Connie was involved
with each kid. It wasn't a thing where she addressed the group in
general; each child had individual attention. I had never seen that.

Natasha Blake adds: "It may have been a class of 20 something, but you
just didn't feel like you were in a crowd. The teacher was there for you and
you alone, as well as the person who sat next to you."
Teachers not only paid attention to each student individually, but
treated each one with respect, according to Bessie Blake, Natasha's mother.

The teachers talked to the children like they were people, not just
pupils that had to sit down and follow rules and regulations, and
not really express themselves because there wasn't enough time,
with 40 children in a class. It wasn't like that. They took time with
those children. They treated them as people.

When adults at CPE looked at children, they did not simply see academic learners in need of intellectual growth, but full human beings, with
all the needs and feelings humans have. Evelyn Johnson, herself a teacher
at another East Harlem school, thinks of this difference as "CPE's sense of
humanity."

At another school, if the parents are 15 minutes late picking up the
children after school, they take them to the [police] precinct. Think
of the terror in the child's heart. At CPE, a teacher would stand out
there with you. I remember once, my daughter Ali got left behind;
there was a mixup. She was about 6 when this happened. Debbie
took Ali home. I found out she was at Debbie's house and I was
able to pick her up. Taking children to a police precinct, that's so
inhumane. In my school, when kids get sick, they sit on the bench
and wait for the parent. It hurts me still, because I know at CPE,
when the kids are sick, they find a little cot. They'd cover them up
and give them whatever was necessary. To see a child sitting up on
a hard wooden bench, riding a temperature of 103 and looking
miserable, cuts me to the quick in my own school.

"CPE's sense of humanity" meant that the school took seriously many student needs that most schools define as outside their domain. Take, for example, the issue of nutrition. Vicki Pittman remembers "Junk Free June. We had no candy during that month, just vegetables and fruits."

The snacks children cooked in the afternoon, according to Heather Bush, "were always really natural things. . . . It wasn't brownies, it was carrot cakes and zucchini bread." Natasha Blake says CPE's focus on nutrition had a long-term impact: "In high school, we would all bring our lunch. Everybody's lunch was a big hero, but I would have all these different kind of vegetables."

Another example was the attention CPE gave to students' need to relax, have fun, and explore new worlds on their own. Graduates remember recess in the playground, frequent walks in Central Park, weekly visits to the skating rink, and trips to rural campsites. While teachers took the opportunity to infuse these activities with academic challenges, they also gave students lots of freedom.

For many graduates, these opportunities to find free time and space away from home were especially important because daily life in East Harlem and Harlem had to be severely restricted in the interest of safety or family financial limitations. Greg Powers, who grew up in public housing several blocks from CPE, made this point:

> We used to go camping upstate every year, for 3 or 4 days out of the week. We'd leave on Tuesday night or Wednesday morning, come back Friday. It meant a lot to explore wildlife and nature. Also, it was important to get away, to have a break. That was the only time I got out of the city.

Carmen San Jose seconded Greg, although she had more reservations about CPE's camping trips. When I asked Carmen if she got out much outside of school, she answered:

> Are you crazy? I had to go home because my mother was always watching me, because I was always sick. She had to be able to sit and actually see me playing. The camping trips were fun. I wish she could have come with me. I was scared. It was fun, but I was scared because I'd never been anywhere out alone. What I didn't like at all was the rowboating, getting in the water or swimming, because I was scared of drowning. But other than that, I had a good time playing games and stuff like that.

Marlo Jones shared Greg's and Carmen's sense that CPE gave her freedom that she couldn't have at home in the South Bronx, where her family lived.

> My mother was very cautious. If there was someone that I wanted to play outside with, she would want to see who they are. She would familiarize herself with the people that lived on our block, because outside our block I didn't really associate with anyone. She kept an eye out for things that we did. When I rode the bike, I couldn't ride outside the block.
>
> CPE was the first time I got to have real, regular fun. I had just gotten into my preteens and you start doing a lot of things. One morning we went to Central Park. We couldn't go too far, but we kind of could wander off by ourselves, just have fun. That was all, playing "catch a kiss" and all that stuff. The boys and the girls could socialize! That was fun. You know, just you and a friend want to walk around, you could walk around.

For Gerard Sherman, nature walks in Central Park led to a lifelong interest and plans for a career.

> We went outside a lot. One time when we went to Central Park, we followed a stream running east to west along 110th Street. We followed that and went to some of the back trails with the park ranger. My interest in the outdoors started at CPE.

In New York, Gerard has worked with Inner City Outings, helping children who "normally wouldn't have a chance to get out and do camping and hiking." He plans to work in outdoor recreation when he completes his college degree in that field.

CPE's sense of humanity also was expressed in the effort adults made to give children a chance to enjoy physical play and sports during recess and after school. Jasmine Stevens describes recess as a realm of freedom where she could let loose.

> I liked going out for recess because they didn't plan activities for you to do out there. If you wanted to sit in a corner with a book, you could do that for the whole time. If you wanted to play jump rope, you could. If you wanted to talk with a group of friends and with the guys and joke around, you could. It was just your free period to do whatever you wanted. When you had recess, you

could run wild and let out everything. I liked to be outside in that big yard. I guess it is probably really little, but when I was little, it seemed like it was miles and miles long, and you could run and scream and yell and no one ever told you to be quiet.

Russ and Bruce stand out as being particularly interested in promoting athletics. David Tomas remembers one activity in particular that Russ organized: "Every Friday, after school, we'd go to play at the Y. That was a fun thing to do at the time." Daniel Lopez remembers jogging in Central Park with Bruce and "students that were pretty close to Bruce. Steve Hernandez wasn't in our class, but he always hung around. Robert Mata, I remember, Michael Rodriguez, and a few of the girls. We had a little group of our own."

Other teachers organized trips to Central Park's ice skating rinks. Valerie Sanchez remembers, "in the winter, every week, we would go ice skating. I learned to ice skate there, in CPE. I love it. My mother used to go with us."

Finally, CPE personnel went far beyond the boundaries of the school in caring for and nurturing their students, by accepting responsibility for children beyond normal school hours.

For Mrs. Powers, this expanded conception of the school's responsibility felt like

> a lot of support. I do remember one time I was sick, and I wasn't able to take [my three children] to the bus stop to go to school, so I kept them home 2 days. Debbie called and asked, "What is the matter? Where are those Powers children?" I told her that I wasn't able to get to the bus, I was in bed ill. They came and got those kids. Every day they used to get them and bring them home. They took turns. . . . They would call me and tell me that they would be upstairs soon. There was a support system there. That's something parents really do need.

In addition, the schools' expansive sense of responsibility led personnel to continue their relationships with students outside school. When Tosha was miserable because of family problems, Russ would take her to his home. Jasmine Stevens remembers Russ inviting her to his house—not because she was feeling down, but because he was "really friendly."

When Bruce drove Marla Baker home from school, he gave her more than just a lift—he offered her the opportunity to form close bonds, which she sorely needed.

> I had a lot of problems with my mother. My journals from sixth grade are just filled with, "I hate her; she doesn't even know if I'm

alive." Bruce would read them and we would have these long talks about them. . . . Bruce was committed to what he was doing. I didn't feel like when school ended, he ended. . . . He became a father for me, because I wasn't seeing my father.

Finally, the teachers' concern for students was manifest in the extra effort they put into helping them find additional resources. Mrs. Blake put it this way:

The school encouraged the parents. They made the children take all the tests to go to the best school they could go to, where they didn't have to pay. They let your child take the test to see if they could get a scholarship.

Barbara Martinez benefited from the school's efforts.

Through Alice, we found out about this enrichment program, which helped get us better knowledge about what kind of schools were available to me and my brother. We went in the summer before sixth grade. It was at St. Aloysious in Harlem, on 137th Street. . . . I wouldn't have gone to Brown if it hadn't been for the [help I received there].

But it wasn't only "gifted" students who gained from the teachers' extra concern. Greg Powers said:

The teachers followed up on the kids. They didn't let the children graduate from elementary school and just pop them into a junior high school. They explored the junior high schools until they found the one that suited that particular individual. It was a nurturing situation.

SELF-ESTEEM

Graduates ranked "self-esteem" as being the second most important thing they gained from CPE after "getting along with people." Analysis of the interviews suggests that what graduates meant by this is that CPE helped them foster a sense of who they were and what they valued and believed. Rather than keeping silent in order to protect themselves from a disrespectful and threatening world, rather than conforming to peer pressures, CPE graduates felt they could express themselves freely, open themselves to new experiences and people, ask questions of those in authority, and work and live independently.

Openness

When people feel threatened, they may protect themselves by closing themselves off from the threat in a variety of ways. They may keep hidden thoughts and feelings that they think will be judged unacceptable by those in authority. In a classroom, this may mean never volunteering answers, or telling teachers what they want to hear. Students may try literally to hide from the teacher by avoiding eye contact, by sitting in the back of the room, or by crouching behind other students. Students also may give only terse, even monosyllabic, answers.

Students also may attempt to protect themselves by ignoring people they perceive as uncaring or threatening. If they think that they cannot learn new material successfully, or in the way the teacher expects, they may choose not to listen at all. If they think that the teacher will not respect their answers or opinions, they may make no effort, or try only to figure out what the teacher wants to hear. Herbert Kohl (1991) has written about inner-city children who make no effort or, in Kohl's terms, tell the teacher, "I won't learn from you." Equally common is regurgitating the teacher's lectures without understanding them.

When CPE graduates talked about what they had gained from attending CPE I and CPE II, they frequently said that the loving and respectful manner in which school personnel related to them—as well as the curriculum's emphasis on expressiveness in journal writing, fiction writing, musical performance, and fine arts—enabled them to be open in both the sense of expressing their thoughts, feelings, and emotions, and in the sense of taking in new ideas and information.

Jasmine Stevens and her grandmother agreed that Jasmine became more expressive as a result of her experiences at CPE. Jasmine is now a self-assured, assertive young woman training to be a teacher, and ultimately a school administrator, but before she began attending CPE, Jasmine's grandmother remembers her as being withdrawn. While she was at CPE, Jasmine became quite outspoken, her grandmother says:

> I learned that when she graduated out of CPE, and I heard her speak at her commencement. I was shocked. I sat there that day, and thought, "Well, she's going places." . . . Since I've been around Jasmine, she's taught me a little. I speak up for myself now.

By the time Jasmine was in junior high school, she had enough confidence to challenge her teacher when she felt the teacher was placing her in the wrong class. Jasmine believes her experience at CPE made it possible for her to confront her teacher at East Harlem Performing Arts.

> That's another part of CPE, helping you express your ideas on things, not feeling that your environment is so strict that you can't express when you feel something. At CPE, they encouraged you to express yourself, if something was bothering you. Debbie Meier always said, "Come to my office and talk about it." So [in junior high school] I wrote this long letter about how I didn't like the fact that I couldn't go in the other [math] class. I told [my teacher] that if she wanted to see if I could do the work, she should give me tests that the other class took. I said, "If I don't do well, then I'll stay back." It took a while to convince her to do it, but she did it, and I got excellent grades on these tests, so I went into the next class in the middle of the year.

David Tomas spoke about how the loving and respectful teacher–student relationships at CPE helped him open up to new ideas. David had a hard time taking in anything from the school at first.

> To listen to a teacher that wasn't my mother or my father, to me, that person was not an authoritative figure. It wasn't somebody I felt I had to listen to. I had to break that home habit of "just listen to mommy and daddy and that's it."

When I asked David what that enabled him to start paying attention to his teachers, his immediate response was to mention activities like building ships, and trips to the nearby sand park, or to the way projects were done in conjunction with curriculum themes. But then David stopped talking about CPE's specific academic methods and turned to the nurturing emotional environment: "I feel that in CPE, the teachers really cared about the students. They put in the extra effort because they cared."

While David had terrible problems in junior high and high school, he earned his GED, he's working, and he's trying to support his son. David believes that CPE's nurturing has had a long-lasting effect on the person he is. When I asked him what would have happened had he gone to a more traditional elementary school, he answered:

> I believe I might have been a different person now. I don't think I would be as understanding as I am now. I would just be a normal

kid, just another number, just another Hispanic. That's it. I feel like I'm a little more than that, not that I'm better than anybody else, but I feel that as a person, I'm a little more, because of Central Park East. More able to look at things in a different way, not seeing things one way. Taking certain situations and thinking about them in a different way. It broadened my mind and made me really think about what I was doing. CPE succeeded in opening up my mind more than any other school would have done. . . . It's almost scary to think what would have happened if I was in an ordinary elementary school.

Asking Questions

Years ago, when I was writing the history of the CPE schools, I spoke to the principal of an East Harlem junior high school that admitted many CPE graduates. As soon as I mentioned CPE, a smile lit up his face. "You can always tell the kids that went to CPE," he told me. "They don't accept anything you tell them at face value. They're always asking, 'Why?' They're the most demanding students we've ever had."

In traditional classrooms, many factors discourage students from asking questions. First, when teachers lecture students on the material that will be included on state-mandated tests, they often discourage students from asking questions because of the year-long rush to "cover" the curriculum. Second, many students fear that asking questions is a confession of ignorance; it's safer to hide their uncertainty or confusion. Third, many teachers act as if a student's question is a challenge to their authority; they may belittle the student who dares to ask why.

But teachers at Central Park East did not lecture, nor did they "cover" prescribed curriculum; rather than discourage students from asking questions, they welcomed the active assertion of student interest and curiosity. Moreover, because they did not claim complete control of student activity, they tended not to view student questions as a threat to their authority. Anessa Boland put it well.

In CPE and in my junior high school, I asked a lot of questions. I was worse than a 3-year-old with that constant why. When I asked why, I asked specifics. . . . They came to expect that in CPE and it helped a lot. . . . That was something I really liked about Bruce. He would admit he would not know something. That was one thing that really endeared Bruce to me. He would look at me funny, and say, "I don't know. Let's go find out."

But the fact that CPE graduates felt free to question their teachers rested on more than the fact that CPE valued students' questions; CPE also nurtured the graduates' self-esteem so that they weren't afraid to ask those questions in the first place. Heather Bush, who has completed a Master of Arts degree in psychology, and plans to become a school psychologist, says that she was a "quiet kid," but CPE helped her to

> overcome the shyness enough to ask questions, and the teachers were receptive to it. Connie and Alice always had time for questions. Even if it had nothing to do with what you were doing, they'd answer your questions, and they'd help you find resources.

Reaching Out

Throughout their descriptions of their paths to academic growth and success, graduates recounted how their positive feelings about themselves enabled them to reach out to adults for help in ways children more conflicted in their relationships with authority have trouble doing.

Marla Baker, whose close relationship with Bruce in sixth grade was described earlier, continued to benefit from warm, trusting relationships with teachers at Columbia Prep and Wesleyan College.

> At any place, you find a few teachers that you really like. Those are the people that are going to be with you for a long time and encourage you. I had a few of those teachers who were wonderful, and whom, I felt, when I graduated, I was very good friends with. At Columbia Prep, for example, one professor was my mentor. He taught me everything about South Africa, and Latin America, and Freud, everything.

Not only was Marla able to form helpful relationships with teachers outside CPE, but her close friendship with Bruce Kanze continues. On the day I interviewed Marla, she was making plans to

> see Bruce all day at CPE, which I'm really excited about. I'm going to stay in Bruce's class all day, go out to lunch maybe. It's going to be weird. I'm in this Educational Studies class and I want to go write a paper on CPE, on progressive education.

Afterwards, she described her feelings about the visit.

I was talking to my mother about it. I was telling her that I have just had the most beautiful day. I was so happy. I just started crying because it made me feel so good. In a lot of ways, it made me think I wanted to be a teacher even more than I thought I did before. It was great to go back there.

Independence

Developing a strong sense of her ability to work and live independently freed Marla to form close relationships with adults in positions of authority. CPE attempted to instill this same sense of independence in all students in several different ways. One was CPE's teaching practice, in which teachers acted as coaches, or guides, rather than instructors. For example, as Marlo Jones tells us, when describing Alice's fifth/sixth-grade class:

Homework assignments would be on a couple of pages; it would be on a range of subjects. [Alice] would give it to us and say that it was to be handed back in a couple of days. You were responsible for that. We might get a reminder but it was basically your responsibility to do this homework. It wasn't checked everyday. Maybe if you had a problem you could ask her about it. I thought that was pretty cool. It was up to me whether or not I waited until Sunday night or did it during the week.

Cheryl DeSilver remembers:

We had so much freedom. Responsibility was put on us to get the work done on our own. When it came later, in junior high school, I was self-motivated. I didn't have to have any supervision. I don't remember my mother checking my homework. . . . Challenges were great. I loved them. I didn't like doing really easy stuff.

Other aspects of CPE reinforced the impact of the schools' teaching methods on creating the children's sense of independence. Kathy Title cited the relationships fostered between older and younger children.

We were allowed to go down and help with the younger kids so it made you feel like you had responsibility to look out for them. You felt independent in being able to do it and you felt much more self-confidence. [The teachers] built upon it.

Mrs. Powers and her son Greg add that CPE's curriculum and structure were additional ingredients in creating the graduates' independence. According to Mrs. Powers:

> They taught students the basics of life. Greg could cook; he could sew. Those are some of the things we really do need. For me, being a parent and working, sometimes I just didn't have a lot of time to focus in on areas that my kids could use. . . . The structure of the school made me feel comfortable leaving them, knowing that they knew not to open the door to strangers. I think the structure of the school did a great deal of teaching.

Greg adds:

> When I was in the third and fourth grade, I used to come home with my sister by ourselves. We knew what we had to do, that our mother wasn't home. We had our priorities set; we had to clean up, do our homework, and wait for our mother to get home.

GETTING ALONG WITH PEOPLE

Kids at CPE were close, like a family, brothers and sisters. There were a few fights but the fights were just moments of heated anger. You get angry with everyone at one time or another, but nothing really went on after that.
(Alvin Ortiz)

CPE helped their students to be moral: "Don't ever be intimidated to do things that you want to do, as long as you're not going to do them maliciously." They make you feel as if it's a family. They taught us we're all in the same situation. We're all people, so we should treat each other the way you would expect someone to treat you.
(Steve Hernandez)

Everybody had the same teachers, and everybody was treated with respect. There were a couple of bad kids, but they weren't so bad all the time, and there wasn't fighting. After lunch, we went and sang. You can't hate people you sing with.
(Heather Bush)

Graduates ranked "getting along with people" as the single most important thing they gained from CPE, and "respect for others" as third most important. When interviewed, graduates stressed that CPE, as a complex whole, and in its individual classrooms, enabled them to develop socially in three important ways: (1) they formed close friendships with other students; (2) they gained a sense of responsibility for other members of the school family; and (3) they gained self-discipline as they internalized their responsibility to others.

Friendships

Many CPE graduates believe that they formed friendships with more of the students in their classes than is usually the case in other schools; their friendships were closer and warmer than usual, and their childhood friendships lasted longer than usual. In fact, half the graduates surveyed when they were 18–23 years old said that they were still friends with former classmates from CPE.

As Barbara Martinez noticed when she was student teaching, the way students worked together interdependently caused them to "know more about what is going on in their classroom."

The noncompetitive tone established by teachers in the classroom permeated relationships between students as well, so much so that many students used the phrase, "We were like brothers and sisters." Lola Johnson went further.

> My friends were really my friends. I really liked them. It wasn't like, "Three o'clock, boy, I'm glad to get out of here." My best friend now, Yvonne, she went from CPE all the way up. And Carol also, and Robert and Michael. I still speak to all of them, really.

CPE encouraged the development of close relationships outside school by giving all members of the school community a directory of telephone numbers and addresses. Alvin Ortiz says:

> I used to call JoJo at home to discuss a project in school that we were working on. A lot of kids that I know from my neighborhood, they wouldn't call their other classmates; a lot of them didn't even have their numbers, but at CPE, every year, you'd have a directory of everyone's parents. You would be free to call them.

Although CPE students traveled to school from all over Manhattan and beyond, they often visited each other's homes after class. Greg Powers remembers:

We really used to all hang together. We were really tight-bonded. We stuck together. . . . Out of school, or during the weekend, we might go to different people's houses. Like everybody may come to my house one weekend. We may go to our friend Robert's house or David's house. We stayed together.

Daniel Lopez adds:

My best friend was Jimmy O'Rourke. He was my best friend all through elementary school. I hung out with him and brought him into the crowd. I went to his house, and I stayed over. I met his father, and his father's girlfriend. I stayed over there about three times.

Likewise, Natasha Blake's mother recalls, "I had everybody's kids over at my house. They would come over and play with Natasha. I just felt better about it, because Natasha was the only child. This way she had somebody to play with."

Children, of course, are not all sugar and spice; forming and reforming cliques, making fun of classmates, jockeying for power and prestige, even downright cruelty are part of any real story of childhood, and CPE graduates had vivid memories of giving and receiving.

Carol Hall, who entered CPE in fourth grade, remembers her first day at school.

We went up to the gym. It was recess, and they were playing with this huge ball. I'm standing there by myself. I had all these curls in my hair. Lola came over to meet me. She pulled my hair and ran back to her friends. So I turned around, and, dumb me, I asked this other girl, Nicole Shoulders, "Did you pull my hair?" What was I going to do if she told me yes? And she looked at me and she said, "No." That's what I remember; these girls pulled my hair. I couldn't believe it. And then she did it again. I thought, "I don't believe this." I was a timid kid. I wasn't a fighter. I was in a book all the time. I wasn't one to say, "Look, cut it out." I never had that problem in my neighborhood. . . .

The older kids at CPE were the bullies; that's the way I saw them. I was always more of a follower, because I wasn't one to speak up. I was always going along with the crowd, not getting into trouble, just doing things that I wasn't the leader.

I wound up becoming friends with these girls. When I went to junior high school, Lola and I were really close.

Responsibility

> If a kid had a problem, we all had a problem. We all shared whatever happened to us. When somebody's mother died, we were all involved. When it came to fund raising for a certain person, we all had to get involved.
> (Stephanie Gonzalez)

Although memories of teasing and bullying abound in the graduates' interviews, more common are stories about students helping each other, supporting each other, sharing with each other, and taking turns.

CPE's educational program necessitated that students develop a sense of responsibility for each other. In an "open" classroom, students are far more interdependent than in a classroom where the teacher is always in front of the room directing the students' learning. When one group of students is working with the teacher on arithmetic problems while other students are reading silently, chaos can prevail if students don't learn to respect each other's needs.

CPE staff tried to create order in the classroom not through imposition of adult authority, but by teaching students to understand their responsibility to others. For example, when Lola was bothering another student, Bruce didn't yell, nor did he rush to punish her. Instead, he appealed to Lola's sense of responsibility to her classmate and her classmate's mother, as well as for Bruce's own well-being. Lola confesses:

> We used to terrorize one of the girls because she was new to the classroom. I don't know why we did it, but we used to really bother her. Debbie wanted to suspend me, and Bruce said, "Lola, I am out on the limb with you. Please, I've run out of excuses. You really have to shape up. I'm fighting to keep you from being suspended this one time, but I really cannot take you back anymore." I said, "Okay." And I stopped.

Jasmine Stevens, who had no siblings at home, describes her social development at CPE as a process by which she learned at school what she didn't have the opportunity to learn at home. "Being up here, I didn't have to share with anybody, so when I got down there, I learned to share. There was a lot of sharing going on at CPE. They provided animals and cooking. So it was a very sharing atmosphere."

Later in her interview, Jasmine described how Johnny Stein and Mark Silver helped her learn the computer. And when Jasmine wasn't busy learning from her fellow students, she was trying to teach them.

> Alice would have us read three or four pages out loud. I liked doing that, because I liked being the teacher. If I could teach someone

something, I would run to the board with chalk. I wouldn't do it on paper, because I liked being the teacher. So if I got to read, I would try to read as clear as possible, without any mistakes, because it made me feel as if I was teacher.

As a teenager, Jasmine's interest in helping people developed further. As a member of the International Club, she organized a food drive for the homeless. And at the Minisink Townhouse, a community center, she taught her peers about sex and personal responsibility.

Basically just helping people. I think if you can help someone to do better and it's not going to make you go out of your way, if it's not going to stop you from what you're doing, also, then by all means do it. If you're sitting at home all day for hours and hours, watching television, then just an hour could help somebody else do something. We also did tutoring. I tutored a girl that was in the seventh grade in biology. . . . It wasn't a political interest at all. Sometimes you just feel the need to do something for people.

Self-Discipline

Nicole was a bully. She beat me up. Vicki Pittman, also, they all jumped in on me. I was playing kick ball. It was outside in the yard, and Vicki started the whole thing. I think she wanted to be on my team or something like that, and I said, "I don't know." She hit me for no reason, like pushed me against the gates, so I hit her back, and the next thing I knew, four or five girls came and they weren't crazy about me. . . . Later, Nicole became like a sister to me. We were just growing up. That's all it was, just kids.
(Tosha Prince)

Of course, CPE students did not always act considerately or responsibly toward one another. The staff's response was to treat students with respect rather than a heavy hand, hoping they would internalize rules of decent behavior, rather than just submit to external authority. While CPE's approach was not consistent, or always effective, most graduates believed that CPE students became noticeably better behaved than students at other schools with which they were familiar.

Lola Johnson and her mother told a story about CPE's disciplinary process that probably comes close to the school's ideal approach. Before she came to CPE, Lola was a terror, acting out in response to family troubles. In her kindergarten class she got in trouble so often that her desk was placed near the principal's office. Later, when she began attending CPE, things gradually changed.

At CPE, I never really got punished a lot, because the good things I did were focused on instead of the bad things. I remember one time, we were in the schoolyard and this guy, Johnny, he had the frisbee and he wouldn't give it to me. I said, "Give me the frisbee." And he wouldn't give it to me or throw it to me so I grabbed his hand and I bit it and I wouldn't let it go. I saw it turning blue and everything. Russ came and he was furious. He said, "What happened? Do you see his hand?" I said, "Yep, we were throwing frisbees; he wouldn't let me have it, so I bit him." And he says, "That's not the way you handle things; you come to me." I had to explain to Johnny's mother why I bit him. She was furious. And I was wrong. I was scared because I thought, "Okay, I really am wrong." There's not much more I could do because I have to face his mom on my own. But it was more like they heard you out. With the reputation that I had, I had a fair hearing always. I wasn't always accused. Things went wrong, it wasn't, "Lola, you were in the wrong, what did you do now?" It wasn't like that. It was, "What happened?" Most of the time it wasn't me, it was somebody else.

At CPE we used to learn that if you didn't see something as being right, explain why. When I used to get in trouble in CPE, Bruce used to say, "Okay, am I wrong for not letting you go to recess?" I used to have to say, "No, you're not wrong, because it was my fault." But if I felt he was wrong, I had the right to say, "Well yes, you are wrong, because it wasn't my fault." And he'd sit there. All the teachers were like that. They would sit and listen to you. It was like a trial. If you can prove to them that you weren't wrong, you can go to recess, if it really wasn't your fault.

They wanted to hear what happened. You explained in a story. You can say, "I was wrong," or, "He stuck his tongue out at me and I tripped him." And then you're hearing yourself say this and you're thinking, "I was wrong and I'm ready to accept my punishment." It's not like they just come in and say, "I saw you trip him, it was your fault; recess is taken away from you for 3 days." It was more like, "I'm wrong, I'm ready to accept the punishment." They didn't yell at you. They weren't yelling, "What's the matter with you? What are you, crazy?"

Graduates also recalled times when CPE's disciplinary process didn't work so well. Anessa Boland, who was young, short, and chubby, was teased mercilessly by classmates, and when Bruce couldn't stop the teasing, or stop it from bothering Anessa, fighting erupted.

The only thing Bruce handled badly, in my opinion, was when the girls used to tease me and really hurt me. The one thing he said was, "They don't mean it. They're just teasing." It used to hurt me because I wanted these people to accept me. I thought of them as my friends and then they would turn around and tease me and I would be crying and they'd keep it up. They would think it was funny. I didn't think it was funny at all. Bruce would say, "Oh, they don't mean it. They're just having fun." I didn't know how to tease them back.

Other graduates told me that sometimes teachers imposed discipline in a heavy-handed manner. Mrs. Bankhead took her children out of CPE in part because she thought the school was sending one of her sons out of the classroom too often.

Every time he would get into trouble, they would make him come down and sit right by the office. A lot of days, he would be there all day long. I thought that was wrong. It got so bad that Deborah wanted to bring a counselor in and have a talk with everybody and see what they could do to help my son. When she brought him in, they told him how my boy's behavior was. He wanted to know how they dealt with it. And almost in every way this counselor told them they were wrong. "You don't take a child and just sit him right down here, all day long," he said. "Let him go in the gym and work some of it off." I was so glad she called that conference because I knew what I had told them, and it worked out just beautiful. But later, I took him out anyway. . . . My son did have a problem; your problems don't just leave you like that. In almost every school he went to, he had problems, but there were teachers who understood and dealt with him.

The counselor Mrs. Bankhead refers to came from the Ackerman Institute. He suggested that the school adopt a "family conference" process to bring together teachers, students, and parents to talk about how the school environment could be modified so that the child would be able to function more effectively. Family conferences reinforced CPE's practice of respecting the student, by making it a clear rule that it was not to be assumed that the child was wrong, nor were adults to talk behind his or her back. The adoption of the family conference approach to discipline is a key example of how CPE solved problems not by hiding them or by blaming the victim, as so many institutions do, but instead by developing more effective practices.

While the graduates said that CPE never fully resolved the issue of discipline, many former students and their parents agreed that CPE students learned to discipline themselves, and to get along with others, noticeably better than others in the same age group.

Mrs. Powers, who lived several blocks from the school, told me, "I can always tell children that came from CPE. From their behavior, how they conduct themselves, at the bus stop, or in the grocery store. I could just tell they came from CPE."

Alvin Ortiz, who traveled to CPE from the Lower East Side, agreed.

When I used to go on my way to school, past public school, I would see kids that were out in the yard, playing games and acting in a different way. When you go to CPE, most of the kids were already in the building, not loitering outside. That was different. I think that they were just more respectful to the teachers, because of the relationships they had.

Stephanie Gonzalez, who lives across the street from the old CPE building, adds:

Parents have seen the way the kids have been brought up in CPE, compared to the way their kids were brought up in another school. Look where the school is. I haven't seen any problems or any type of fighting or any wild riots at CPE. I've seen other schools around here where there were crazy riots, but I never saw that at CPE. Police officers or ambulances in front of the school? Never, never.

Finally, Steve Hernandez contrasts the behavior of CPE students favorably with that of parochial school students he knew in East Harlem.

Kids who went to parochial school were hit with a ruler. I don't think that it worked at all. I feel the majority of the people who went to those schools didn't come out the way they should have. It's weird. I see drugs, young pregnancies. I have yet to see someone from CPE really into drugs or young pregnancies, things like that. I see it a lot from kids who went to parochial schools.

CONCLUSION

"School" at CPE was more than just an academic institution, and "progress" was never limited solely to the academic sphere. The intimate, safe environment at CPE, its homey classrooms, and its respectful and loving staff enabled students to gain a sense of trust for adults, for their fellow students, and for themselves. Self-respect blossomed into self-esteem and self-discipline, while respect for others led to long-lasting friendships.

Graduates and their parents often referred to CPE as a "family," and like all families, it was full of conflict and strife, cliques and jealousies, fights and cruelty. But virtually without exception, graduates believed that CPE's nurturing environment promoted their social and emotional growth.

NOTE—THE TEENAGE PREGNANCY ISSUE

Steve's comments about "young pregnancies" opens up a complicated issue. The teachers and parents who participated in designing the survey agreed with Steve that teenage pregnancy is a symptom of social and personal disorder. It is for this reason that the survey included a question about whether the graduates had children—many of the parents and teachers who participated in designing the survey believed that if CPE was successful in helping its graduates achieve social and emotional growth, that success would be reflected in a low rate of teenage pregnancy. Although I disagreed with this belief, I included questions in the survey about whether graduates had children.

When I asked students whether they had children, many of them scoffed in response and then explained that for them a youthful pregnancy would represent a setback in their plans for a successful career and life. For example, Vicki Pittman told me:

> I know from my own point of view, I'm not ready physically, mentally, or financially for a baby. . . . It's hard to work full time, go to school full time or part time, and come home and take care of a baby. That's a full-time job too. Right now, it's something that I don't want and I'm not ready for.

Clearly, some of the students I interviewed, such as Vicki, seem to share the belief of the teachers and parents that teenage pregnancy is a symptom of pathology. Vicki continued:

> Those who mean to have a baby but don't really have anything to offer that child, I think that it's just a matter of having low self-esteem. It's a matter of being stupid, thinking that if I have this man's baby, it's going to keep him here. But eventually, as they

seem to wise up, they realize, "He's still not here." So obviously this baby did not keep him here.

Conversely, for Vicki, avoiding teenage pregnancy is a sign of maturity.

> When I talk to a lot of adults, and they hear the way I talk about things, they say, "I'm surprised to hear it coming out of your mouth, to be so young." . . . Due to the fact that I was always a straightforward, outspoken person, I had no problem with telling the boys, "This is what I'm going to do and this is what I'm not going to do, and you can either accept it or decline, that's your choice." It was never a problem where I felt like I was in a jam, or being pressured into doing something I didn't want to do. As far as peer pressures with friends or with a male–female relationship, those two things I never had a problem with, feeling peer pressure to do anything I didn't want to do.

But when I spoke to the graduates who had children, it was clear that while having a child when they were young made it harder for them to achieve their goals for education and employment, and in addition brought them disapproval, they did not believe that having a child was a sign that they were lacking in morality or maturity. They still had strong self-esteem and still believed they would make something of themselves. For example, Stephanie Gonzalez, who was 21, and on maternity leave from her job at Xerox when I interviewed her, told me:

> I do feel good about myself. . . . I am not embarrassed. Yes, I am Puerto Rican; yes, I'm having a baby; but I don't see myself as being like other people around here. It's sad, and it's a shame, but what's important is whatever you have up here [in your head], how you carry yourself.

Kathy Title, who became pregnant while she was a first-year student in an Ivy League college, has a similar outlook.

> It never seemed like, "What am I going to do after I have this baby?" I always thought that somehow this was just going to make the trip a little longer. But I would still make it to whatever I was going to do, and I was going to be successful at it.

And that has happened for Kathy. She is still with the father of her babies, she is in a corporate management training program at a Fortune 500 company, and she earns far more than most people of her age, 24. So, for Kathy, and for other graduates, having a baby does not seem to be a symptom of poor self-esteem.

While I do not share the assumptions that are embedded in the survey questions I asked about whether the graduates had children, I present the data that I collected. At most, 9 of 112 CPE graduates had children (8%) while they were unmarried teenagers. One was male (out of 48, or 2.1%), and eight female (of 64, or 12.5%). Four of 29 female CPE graduates of color from East Harlem bore children before they were 20 (13.8%). At this time, in East Harlem as a whole, there were more than 30 live births for every 100 females under age 20, according to the U.S. Census. Thus, the rate of teenage pregnancy for female CPE graduates from East Harlem was less than half the rate for the general population.

❧ 4 ❧

Racial Dimensions of a Learning Community

I had a roommate freshman year; her parents were prejudiced but she wasn't. She grew up in a White neighborhood and she was ignorant about Black people. She used to ask questions like, "Why do you use this shampoo and not that one? Why's your hair like this and not like mine? Do Black people smell different?" My friends couldn't deal with her. They said, "I don't believe it. She should have gotten smacked in the mouth a long time ago. I'm not going to sit here and let her talk like this; I'm leaving. You're crazy. What's the matter with you? Change roommates." But she was trying to learn. She ended up calling one of my Black friends, "my brother." She was really good at heart.

I think that I, coming from CPE, learned there how to deal with her. I wasn't so quick to say, "Are you crazy? I want another roommate. This is intolerable." She just wasn't aware. She was ignorant about different cultures and she wanted to know about them.

(Lola Johnson)

CPE's STUDENT BODY differed from those of most other progressive schools in that it was drawn from a variety of racial groups and socioeconomic strata. How did CPE's social diversity affect its students' social and emotional development?

When CPE was established in 1974, the country's dominant tendency was integrationist—the nation's social goal was to enable people of different backgrounds to interact on an equal plane. Separatism was challenging integrationism, however. A number of White ethnic groups advocated cultural pluralism, an acceptance and valuing of diversity. Within the Black community, racial separatism was a strong, although minority tendency. In New York City, some Black parents, community activists, and educators proclaimed that "community control" of schools was their goal, not access to the mainstream. Within East Harlem, Puerto Rican nationalism was at a peak, and the movement for parent-controlled "bilingual" schools had established several private schools and had influenced the creation of some public schools as well.

CPE emerged distinct from the "community control" and bilingual movements. At its founding, its predominant ethos was integrationist; teachers saw their role as enabling students to respect and tolerate others, to gain access to the traditions of Western culture as well as to gain strengths that would enable them to move into, or perhaps challenge, the mainstream of American society. Over the years, CPE has changed, as teachers, students, parents, and American society also have changed.

But this chapter is not about that process of historical change—a story in its own right. Rather, it concerns how the social diversity of the CPE family affected the way students interacted with their teachers and each other and affected the graduates' formation of their own sense of who they are in relationship to American society.

RELATIONSHIPS

Most CPE graduates said that there was little or no conflict among people of different social backgrounds. In fact, when I asked graduates how children of different backgrounds interacted, most acted surprised that I even asked the question. Steve Hernandez's response was typical: "We never discriminated; it just felt like a family. We didn't have no kind of racial problems, especially that young."

Crossing Racial Boundaries

Beyond the fact that graduates reported little or no prejudice or conflict, most agreed that CPE students mixed regardless of race or class. Marlo Jones, who transferred to CPE from a Catholic school in the Bronx, said, "Where [CPE] is, you can get a good mixture of White, Black, and Spanish. . . . If someone was nice, I got along with him." Cheryl DeSilver, who transferred to CPE from Champ Montessori school in Harlem, agreed.

> I really liked the fact that there was a very even mix; there were some Hispanics and there were some Blacks and Whites. Everything was nicely mixed and that was really good. . . . From the beginning, I thought the kids were really nice.

Strong friendships formed across racial and class lines, according to Lola Johnson, the daughter of a Black man and an Hispanic woman: "I was friends with everybody. . . . If I liked you, I liked you. It had nothing to do with your color or where you came from."

Vicki Pittman, an African American from West Harlem, hung around with three Puerto Rican girls from East Harlem.

> It used always to be us four. I would go to Josephine San Jose's house after school. As we got older, we went ice skating together since it was right there in the area, and I can recall us going to the movies together, the four of us.

While students and parents generally agreed that CPE fostered good relations among people from different backgrounds, there were disagreements about how this came about. Some said that CPE's family-like environment enabled students to preserve the color blindness with which they entered the school, while others argued that the very process of attending CPE was what broke down distrust and prejudice brought to the school.

Lola felt CPE's environment preserved childhood innocence.

> CPE, it's such a utopian place, with all the different colors and different racial backgrounds. . . . I had White friends and Black friends and Spanish friends and Oriental friends. [There were no Asian students in the school when Lola was there.] No one ever said, "You're White or you're Black." It was never like that. I don't even remember things like that. It hit me when I was in junior high school.

Jill Hill, one of the few White students in the early years, agreed: "Growing up on 97th Street, I never really was aware of color differences until my family moved south to Baltimore, where I became very aware of segregation for the first time."

Overcoming Distrust

Within the interviews, however, even those with people who stressed how members of the CPE family were color-blind, there were indications that something more complex occurred, that people who brought to CPE animosities or distrust of those who were different overcame these feelings and learned to love all those in the school family. A story told by Mrs. Powers about how Black students and Hispanic students at CPE came to the defense of Deborah Meier's son, rather than siding with neighborhood Blacks and Hispanics, lends support to this analysis.

We had this big disco at the school. The parents' association didn't want the children to hang out on the weekends, so the parents tried to do something for them where they could get together with proper supervision. The children on the block attacked Debbie's son and his friends [who were attending as guests]. It was really a racial problem. If it had gone on, it would have become a very violent kind of situation. It was so rewarding to see how all the CPE children came to protect Debbie and her family.

Four different CPE graduates told similar stories about how CPE helped students break through social barriers to reach understanding and friendship.

Anessa Boland has lived at Tracy Towers, a high-rise in the Bronx inhabited mostly by African Americans, near Mosholu Parkway and the Bronx High School of Science, since she was 5 years old. She came to Central Park East with "misconceptions" about White people, but that changed, she remembers.

In sixth grade Nancy Wright happened. To me she was one of the strangest people that I ever knew. She was the first person I knew who was not Black who actually liked Blacks, and she surprised me. We got along great. She just turned me around about White people in general, because I used to have my little misconceptions. Then I met Nancy and thought, "She doesn't do this, she doesn't do that; maybe I was all wrong. Maybe what the kids that I grew up with had told me was all wrong."

For Tosha Prince, whose mother is Black and father is White, transferring to CPE from a private school was difficult at first, because her unusual skin color made her a target for the cruelty that so often marks childhood social development. But over time, CPE's emphasis on groupwork helped Tosha and her classmates eliminate the racial component from their social dynamic.

In the very beginning I had a few problems with the Blacks because my mother, who would take me to school, is Black, and I wasn't very dark and my hair was a little lighter. . . . They beat me up a few times. They hadn't yet learned from CPE that color just didn't mean a thing. We all learned that by the time we graduated. . . . I fit in for the first time in my life, because there were so many different ethnic groups, and people of all cultures and classes. . . . I hadn't really grown up with Black or Hispanic kids, because I'd been in private school. I enjoyed finally seeing somebody who looked similar to me, anybody with some color.

When Jasmine Stevens entered Central Park East, she was already aware of White racism, as well as Black anger toward Whites: Her mother had once been expelled from a newly integrated high school for defending herself against some White students who were harassing her. With the help of CPE teachers and classmates, Jasmine learned to open herself to those different from her.

> There was not a bit of racism. I only had one Black teacher, Virginia, and she was just as nice and the White teachers were just as nice. Sometimes you may hear people speak about how White people act; sometimes you are going to run into people who don't trust White people because of past histories; some Black people don't want to interact with Whites. But the White teachers at CPE, they seemed like they were people, not like White or Black, they were just teachers.
>   When I got to Colorado, it was Steamboat Lodge, we were the only Black people there. My mother enrolled us in a ski school, me and my cousins. The adults went off somewhere in the lodge, to drink or see a show or something like that, while we were on the trails; we got treated so badly. It surprised me. That was my first time in that type of atmosphere where we were the only Black people. They didn't want to touch us; we weren't called by our names; we were always together; we never interacted; we never mixed. When they sent the people up on the ski lift, we didn't go. So, I asked, "Why the White people at my school aren't like that, you don't even really know you're different, so how come you're being treated like that here?" My mother explained it to me [about] the way some people are: "You're going to get treated like that, a couple of times before you pass away. That's going to happen a couple of times," she explained to me.

At CPE, Jasmine remembers that she

> met students that taught me something new. Mark was Jewish. I don't think I even knew what a Jewish person was. I had no idea. It wasn't one of those things you tried to find out. One day, he asked me something about myself, and I said, "What are you?" And then he told me, "I'm Jewish," and I said, "What is that?" and then he told me. I said, "Okay, now I know."

Terry Britain, whose mother is White and father is Black, also credits the racial harmony modeled by his teachers at CPE with helping him develop socially.

CPE was the first experience I had with different ways of thinking, with different people. I realized from that experience that different ways could work. And I learned that you could be different and that was fine.

When I was younger, it seemed that the races were very polarized. Maybe that's why I didn't fit in at my traditional public school. At my first public school, I heard a lot of kids talking negatively about White people. There was always this tension, and that's maybe one reason why I didn't fit in. Because, of course, my mother is White. . . . When I went to CPE, race was still somewhat of a factor but not so much. That helped me to forget about that race for a while.

Racial tensions were there. I hung out at CPE with a lot of White kids, and there were Black kids who resented me for that, made comments. But I was having such a good time with my friends. And I saw that the teachers were totally color-blind; that wasn't an issue. They treated all the kids the same. And the Black teachers got along fine with the White teachers; there was never any kind of racial incident. Not having those things was very positive for me.

Confronting Racial Consciousness

While Anessa, Jasmine, Tosha, and Terry describe how CPE helped them overcome racial stereotypes and hostilities they experienced in their neighborhoods, Jimmy O'Rourke says that for him, one of the few White graduates, childhood innocence about racial differences gave way to a painful confrontation with racial consciousness in fifth grade, when he confronted a problem many children have to face when growing up: the loss of close friends. Because the friendships Jimmy made in the integrated environment of CPE were across races, Jimmy's experience of loss took on a racial dimension.

In his first few years at CPE, two of Jimmy's best friends were Kevin and Moses, two Black students who lived in the public housing projects in East Harlem's southeast section. "They were my best friends, and we did everything together." When their family moved uptown and they left CPE, before fifth grade, Jimmy remembers:

I thought it was going to be tough. I think the problem was that for so long, I was White in this Black and Hispanic school, and in a way I didn't really have any White friends. . . . Once Kevin and Moses left, what started happening was that Black friends started

hanging out with Black friends and Puerto Rican friends started
hanging out with Puerto Rican friends. Here I was being White
and I had to mix my way into both, because there wasn't a group
of White kids I could hang out with. Not that things were so
polarized that no one got along, because everyone did, and
everyone played with each other. But everyone started noticing,
"Wait a minute, I'm Black; wait a minute, I'm Puerto Rican; wait a
minute, I'm White. I'm not going to grow an Afro," because that's
what I thought up until fourth grade—at some point, I'd grow an
Afro. But that hit me and shocked me. That put me in a situation
where I really didn't know where to go. . . . For the first time,
somebody called me "White boy." When you haven't had that for
8 years, and all of a sudden someone calls you this, you think,
"I'm not White. Yeah, I am."

    Once they left, I was—not thrown back into the classroom
trying to find new friends, because I knew everybody and we all
hung out, we were in the same classroom all day long—but I had to
readjust to who I was going to hang out with most of the time.

Despite the confusion he experienced, Jimmy came away feeling positive about his relationships with Blacks and Hispanics at CPE.

When I go to my mom's house in Boston, and people start talking
about Black people and other people, I say, "Wait a minute. You
don't know them. You're not friends with them. How can you say
that?" I always felt one step ahead of everyone else. I could catch
them when they didn't know what they were talking about. In that
sense, I'm always listening to what people say, listening to whether
they are right.

This helped Jimmy develop his ability to think critically, "because you had
people from different places and different backgrounds." At Allegheny
College, in a class on Black religion and Black culture,

I had a perspective that not many people had in that class. I wanted
people to know that I'm not as ignorant as they think most White
people are. At the end, I became really good friends with this one
Black woman. We had a great time in the class; we studied outside
the class together. It's been a gradual process but it's been breaking
down barriers the whole way. As I get older, I've been able to go on
and be confident that I can relate to other people.

Opposing Points of View

While most graduates agreed that students of diverse racial and class backgrounds interacted well at CPE, there were dissenters. Heather Bush, herself White, said that there was one clique of two White girls who were horrible together. "They were always together, and Jill was kind of a snob." Jill herself comments: "I had very little in common with the people that went there. Although the children that went there were wonderful, we had very little in common."

Dori Prince, who came to CPE II from Jamaica for fifth grade, was not welcomed to the school. "Because I had an accent; I sounded funny. I had one friend."

Andrea Waller, who transferred to CPE from Champ Montessori school for fourth grade, challenged the notion that CPE students of diverse backgrounds interacted easily and extensively.

> Most people just tended to hang around in groups, divided according to race and economic background. I would hang out with Sabelle, Andrew, Matthew, and Terry, and all of us were pretty much middle class. I remember the Black guys of the class would always hang around with each other. Middle-class Black guys didn't go to CPE. The Black boys who were there, I remember them as being very defensive. I always thought they probably had problems at home, but I don't know. I always thought that they were very angry all the time.
>
> I can only guess at what might have been going on. I think if you come from a poor background and you go to a school where the majority of the people don't really have to worry about much in terms of getting a meal or worry that when you come home, you'll still be in the apartment—when you come home, and you see the luxuries that people have, it will naturally do something to you. I know that Brian did not compromise at all. This is going to be another wild analogy, but I think that's something that a lot of Black men or Black boys are going through. They refuse to compromise, and for better or worse, that seals their fate, because they won't wear the mask. They're just themselves, and that scares people. It scares me to a certain extent, because they won't compromise at all. I remember Brian didn't compromise and he left CPE.

I found Andrea's comments about class and racial differences interesting, so I followed them up when I interviewed other students, but no one confirmed Andrea's notion that Black males from poor or working-class families were isolated at CPE.

CULTURAL IDENTITY

When I turned to how CPE helped students form a sense of cultural identity, I found a wide range of perspectives. Many students placed great value on their experience at CPE because it taught them that "they were as good as everyone else," and because "it opened them up to the opportunities of mainstream American culture."

Joining the Mainstream

Kathy Title, who grew up in a working-class cooperative high-rise project in East Harlem, became an excellent student at CPE after she began studying Black music and history. But she also thinks that CPE's exposing her to "mainstream American culture" was a major contribution to her success.

> I think [your life] is based on what you have been exposed to and what you have seen. I learned that there's another way. My friends in the neighborhood, that didn't see anything past this, they're still here, not working. Some of them have three or four kids and most of them are younger than me and they don't seem like they want anything more. I've met people that are not of my ethnic background that have a lot more to show me or to give to my understanding of what life is about. I've seen that life just isn't this. At CPE, I was exposed to people from different ethnic backgrounds, people who I would have to interact with throughout my entire life. The neighborhood children didn't get that opportunity. They just saw [people like] themselves and that was all there was. Had I not been exposed to this, what would I have done at St. Andrews [Preparatory School]? But I had been. I had established friendships with people of different races, which let me know that I could do it.
>   CPE was a more realistic setting [than my previous school, which was all Black] because you have to encounter different people at every stage of your life. You should be prepared for that. CPE prepared me a lot because I ended up going away to a predominantly White high school. I was a little bit better able to handle it than someone who went to a school that was predominantly Black. . . . At CPE, I had been exposed to not only White teachers

but White students who became friends. For example, I went to spend a night at Heather Bush's house just about every other weekend.

My friends from this community couldn't understand my relationship with Heather, but we had fun. It's important to learn that you can be friends, that race doesn't have to be a barrier.

I got to know her family. Her mom, her dad, and her sister and her brother. I was at the house every weekend. They were probably sick of me. You get exposed to doing different things, like I'd go spend a night at her house, we'd go to the museum, the Metropolitan or the Museum of Natural History. It shows you that there were a lot more things going on than what you see in your community. That's what I think CPE was.

Appreciating Cultural Difference

A second group of students provided a different interpretation of the impact of CPE's harmonious group relations on their cultural identity: They stressed how CPE helped them to appreciate their own cultural tradition, as well as to value cultural differences. Barbara Martinez provided the fullest statement of this perspective.

The teachers did a lot more to learn about us, about your history. One year we studied Africa. I hadn't even thought about Africa before. Puerto Ricans are made up of slaves that came from Africa, but I hadn't thought about that. I thought, this is more than I would have learned if I were reading those little booklets that tell you nothing, where you never see yourself.

We used to say things in Spanish; we had Digna, who everybody liked; we had bilingual teachers, who talked to us in different languages. It wasn't penalized, and it was treated as if it was wonderful to be able to speak a second language. I walked in the Puerto Rican Day parade. I remember making maracas. I loved that. And making a quilt from Puerto Rico. At CPE, you could respect difference; difference was perfectly okay. There was no way that you shouldn't express your difference. Your difference was always wonderful; it was always adding to the class.

Barbara's understanding of cultural differences was reinforced by friendships she had with children from different backgrounds. When Ellen Speth, a White child from the Upper East Side, visited the Martinez apartment in a public housing complex, the clash of cultural protocols produced self-awareness.

> I would invite Ellen over, and she would walk to the refrigerator, open the door, and get something out. My mother thought, "What is going on? In my house, I do that." She never said that to Ellen, but this was a big culture shock. She couldn't believe that this was what people do. . . . It was very different. . . . There were definite cultural differences. . . .
>
> My friends included Latoya and Marlo and Lynette; we used to goof about things and we used to do corn rows with each other's hair, and we used to talk different; the talk was very different than the talk that we would have with Ellen and Jill. At that time, I knew that at Ellen's house, this is how I speak; I knew I spoke differently at Latoya's house.

A Lack of Pride?

A third group of graduates, while positive about CPE generally, argued that the school did not do enough to help students gain pride in their cultural tradition and an understanding of their status in American society.

Cheryl DeSilver, whose father was a member of a Black nationalist literary circle when he attended Howard University, says that it was not until she began to learn about Black history at Howard University that she felt she had missed something important in her earlier education, at CPE.

> I thought that I should have learned this stuff when I was little. I thought these kids need to have the same kind of information, the same kind of feeling of pride and culture that I'm getting now. I should have had it before. It should not have been something that I discovered in college. At least CPE focused on it. The other two schools [I attended] didn't. At least they did put some aspect into it at CPE, but it was like Black history was a lesson, and after we were finished it was over. That would be something that I would change. It wouldn't just be something that you talked about for a month in February and then it was missing in the rest of history. . . . At CPE, at least they paid some kind of attention to it, for an extended period of time, but at Harbor and Worcester [Academy, a private school] there was nothing. If I were at CPE, I would try to incorporate it all, every day. I love the whole CPE curriculum and their whole philosophy, it really fits with what I believe, but to incorpo-

rate Black history into the curriculum. It wouldn't take a whole different curriculum because they already do it so well. [Cheryl began teaching at CPE in 1993.]

I think at age 11, or even younger, children should be getting some sort of sense of identity and what their ancestors have done in particular. Black scientists, what they've done in the past. Some kids don't have any knowledge of any of it.

When I asked Cheryl if she had suffered as a result of not knowing more about the accomplishments of Blacks when she was young, she answered:

I might have, as far as my self-esteem. I didn't even experience racism until after high school, but as far as self-esteem. . . . Because Europeans have this innate sense of self-esteem, because they know they built this country and they know about their ancestors, and where they came from. . . . We can ask an Irish person and they can tell you all about the history of their grandparents and their great-grandparents from Ireland, and how they came where, and what people in their culture have done of significance. I didn't know. . . . As far as me as a Black person, I didn't even think of myself as—I'm Black but that wasn't who I am. Maybe if there had been some cultural pride and some history instilled in me, when I was younger, maybe I might have had more self-esteem.

When I asked Lola Johnson what she thought of Cheryl's thesis, she began to disagree.

We did lots of research on Indians. We did research on Africans, like Egyptians, like King Tut. And we had somebody come in and talk to us about Puerto Rico. With Africa, I remember going to the museum on long tours studying different places in Africa. So, CPE was very multicultural.

But Lola's mother interrupted.

Today, we realize that you have to give them a sense of self before you can move to that ideal. Color blindness is not adequate. It's got to be strong racial pride. Then color blindness can come after that. You have to make sure that kids don't see themselves as inferior, and White as superior. But CPE is better than most places in the sense that they had the books and materials and the curriculum that covers all cultures. In the traditional public school, it's totally lacking; there's nothing.

Terry Britain, when discussing his friendships with White students at CPE, reinforced Cheryl's argument.

I was getting to a point where I started to assimilate to White society and White culture. Because, as far as I saw it, that's who the successful people were. All the minority people I saw weren't doing too well. So I said to myself, "Hey, I can either say that the White people are bad, they're keeping us down, or I can try my best and do all the things that they do to get ahead." . . .

Now I understand that I did try to assimilate to White society, White culture, maybe even more so than was necessary, but that's just a product of the social structure and circumstances. That's the way I got ahead; I was uneducated at the time.

Although Barbara Martinez praised CPE's efforts to teach children to "appreciate difference," she thought the school could have done more to promote her sense of her status within American society.

CPE didn't really teach me how to deal with the way mainstream culture treats minorities because we didn't have a lot of White children there. And I had not really been exposed to all the bad things that happen to people of color. Nowadays, kids know the history of the civil rights movement right on the screen, and they are able to see the violence against women, but it was not obvious to me when I was a kid.

I can honestly say that my sense of identity really didn't develop until I got to college. Obviously something happened before then, but I was not really resistant to the powers that be. It was okay for me to go along with what people wanted me to do. I really didn't question much. It was a cultural thing. I hardly ever disobeyed my mother. I tried to make things very comfortable for her, and it was very comfortable for me. I was a very shy person, and I liked to stay at home.

Because Barbara was generally positive about CPE, I asked her to amplify her comments on cultural identity: "You didn't think of yourself as being a minority?"

I didn't. It's fairly easy to say that because most of the people there were people of color. It's hard to see yourself as a minority, as being the odd person out, when you see people like yourself at home and all around you. . . . We actually learned a lot about how to deal with other people on the outside. So that much I do know I learned; how to deal with other people. But as far as my relationship to the mainstream goes, no. No, in the sense that I couldn't identify that I was a different person from the mainstream; I thought I was a person in the mainstream. I didn't know I was poor until I got to Brown [University]. I knew I didn't have as much money as some people, but I didn't know I was poor. I didn't know that it was such a terrible thing to be Puerto Rican until I got to Cathedral [High School]. But it was when I got back to Brown that I knew what I was; I knew where I had come from; I knew how I learned; I knew who I was in the structure.

Andrea Waller suggests that a shortage of adult role models for minority students at CPE may have contributed to their difficulty in cultural identity formation. (The school had 11 White teachers and only five teachers of color during the years 1978–1983.)

I think the women question actually ties into the race question. I think it was good to have a lot of women teaching, but I just realized that there were no Black male teachers. I don't remember seeing any Black man in the school, ever, no one who was an administrator. I think that that has a subliminal effect on kids, because the only person I saw that I could look up to was Carol. That was probably why we got along so well, because I could identify with her. I really couldn't identify with Debbie or Alice, or anyone else. I think it does have an effect on you when you're growing up and seeing people that don't look like you and they're in charge. I think it did have a subliminal effect on me.

Mrs. Johnson was the only other person I interviewed who agreed with Andrea.

For an East Harlem school, they didn't have very many Black staff members. I think that was one of the weaknesses. They kept giving the children an ideal education, but I think you've got to have a sense of who you are. There was a shortage of Black teachers. So that's a little bit of a problem for a Black child.

CONCLUSION

Aside from a few dissenters, graduates overwhelmingly agreed that in CPE's first decade, there was little social conflict, many students formed friendships across class and racial lines, and many continued to have friendships with peers of diverse backgrounds in secondary school and college.

While most agreed that CPE students mixed well with peers across class and racial lines, there were conflicting ways of interpreting how this came about. Some students painted a picture of childhood innocence preserved in the CPE family; others emphasized how CPE enabled students to overcome prejudices they brought to school.

How racial diversity at CPE contributed to the students' formation of their sense of cultural identity produced even more-varied responses. One group emphasized that CPE promoted their sense that they were "as good as anyone else," and prepared them for life in the mainstream; others stressed that CPE was successful in teaching students to appreciate their special qualities and to value others' differences; and a third group thought that CPE gave insufficient attention to their own cultural identity and social status, leaving them unprepared for later experiences.

These viewpoints differed in emphasis, but they were not mutually exclusive. For example, Kathy Title, who stressed how CPE prepared her for success "in the mainstream," by making her feel that she was "as good as anyone else," also credited the school with helping her gain a sense of identity.

> When I got into CPE, which is culturally mixed to some extent, I started realizing that everybody's not like me. Somehow I had to figure out how to interact in this situation. I realized that when you watch TV, mostly everything that you see is White-oriented. To be in a school like CPE, where if you were interested in Black history, the teachers were the ones that gave you the information that you wanted or you need, that was helpful.

Barbara Martinez, by contrast, both praised CPE's curriculum for creating an "appreciation for difference," and lamented that the school did not confront openly students' minority status.

Nevertheless, despite the overlap in these perspectives, there were differences on one issue: whether CPE helped students to form strong cultural identities that would enable them to cope with the challenges that lay ahead of them. That this should be is not surprising: The issue of cultural identity is one of the most controversial and complex in our society. Debates between advocates of "integrationist," "pluralist," and "separatist" ideologies rage throughout the country and echo in the words of the graduates and their parents.

While there are important disagreements on this matter, they do not overshadow the fact that graduates rated "getting along with people," "self-esteem," and "learning to respect others" as being the most important things they gained from CPE. Furthermore, even those who were critical, often hesitantly so, of this aspect of their experience at CPE, made it clear that they shared CPE's central assumptions about the dignity of all people, the value of cultural diversity, and the importance of appreciating difference.

❧ 5 ❧

"We Bought the Dream": The Parent–School Partnership at Central Park East

When I first wrote about Central Park East back in 1987, I reported that while parents seemed highly pleased with what their children had gained from CPE, many still felt uncomfortable with the school's nontraditional approach to teaching and learning. I attributed this disparity mainly to the fact that CPE's parents were influenced by the dominant society's contrasting ideas about what schools should be like, how children learn, and, above all, what they need to get ahead.

But when I surveyed graduates and parents in 1991, I uncovered more enthusiasm about CPE than I expected. Among the graduates interviewed, 76 of 78 said that their parents liked CPE. And the interviews with parents expressed more appreciation than criticism for CPE's contribution to students' development.

DISSENTERS

Of course, there were some criticisms. The most vehement sprang from Margie Hill, whose two daughters experienced difficulty in Maryland public schools after the family moved from New York City.

> It was a joke. Debbie Meier is a very charismatic person with adults but the kids don't like her. Apparently she's doing something good as far as getting funding into the special program, but kids should not be spending hours making candy and costumes and having parties when they don't know math, they don't know grammar, they don't know any of these things. Some kids came out of the school and did well but those kids would have done well wherever they went. Your average kid who needs basic education did not benefit from the program at all.

While Mrs. Hill's criticism was the harshest, it was not unique. Among the critics were the relatively few who withdrew their children from CPE. Mrs. Cartwright remembers that one man "was very critical of the style [of teaching reading] because he was a teacher in Connecticut. The book at the time was *Why Johnny Can't Read*, and he wanted the kids to learn to read phonetically. Debbie wouldn't relent."

Mrs. Cooper thought the school was beneficial for one daughter, Sabelle, but not for a second daughter, whom she eventually withdrew.

> For Sabelle, CPE was okay. She goes to Mount Holyoke, so that comes from CPE. For the other one, it was not okay because her mind was wandering and the way they taught, "Do what you want to do," she wasn't learning much at all until she was in a structured situation in the fourth grade when I took her out of CPE.

While important to recognize, these negative voices were the exception, not the norm. Most parents said that their first visit to CPE convinced them that this was the right school for their child, and their subsequent experiences only reinforced their enthusiasm.

CPE'S APPEAL TO PARENTS

As mentioned in Chapter 1, when Mrs. Powers discovered CPE in 1974, she was so impressed she decided she wanted her oldest child to go, even though he was already in fourth grade and CPE had no classrooms for children beyond second grade. Mrs. Powers was so determined to have her son attend that, at the suggestion of Debbie Meier, she recruited other parents so that CPE could start a third and fourth grade.

> What really impressed me was the open occupancy of the classrooms, the relaxation of the children, the fact that they were actually using cooking skills and typewriters to learn to spell on and adding machines. I also liked the way that the children were able to relate to the teachers. . . .
>
> When the third and fourth grades started, the teacher, Miss Washington, was really fantastic with these kids. I used to go in and sit around and watch what she did, and participate and did the cooking groups. It branched off from there and it's been booming ever since. I think it's a terrific school.

Mrs. Blake, who lived in West Harlem the entire time her daughter Natasha went to CPE, dates her infatuation with CPE to her first meetings with the teachers in 1974.

> My girlfriend, who babysat for Natasha, and who lived in East Harlem, told me about the school. Our children were among the first to be put into that school. There was only about seven or eight children there at that time. . . . I found that the teachers and Debbie Meier, they were just so real. They were open, and I felt real comfortable around them. They seemed like they cared about our children. They also gave you all the ideas about what they wanted to do with the children in the school. Their main concern was the children.

When I asked Mrs. Blake if the staff's ideas sounded too "radical," she answered:

> No, no, no because it wasn't. They were telling you it wasn't going to be sitting at a desk all in a row and doing strictly this and strictly that. They had a different curriculum set up. It just sounded so good, and they just seemed so nice and caring. It was a different method of teaching the children, and it sounded great to me.

For the Bakers, Gerri and her two daughters, Johnetta and Marla, switching to Central Park East from the beloved Champ Montessori school in West Harlem was not easy. But divorce put Champ out of reach, so the Bakers visited CPE, Mrs. Baker says, hoping to find an affordable alternative.

> Ten minutes before the first classes started, I noticed that the children were having a lot of fun. Then when it was time for classes to start, no adults came and said, "Quiet down." The children simply formed lines. An older child stood at the front of the line and they waited until the kids calmed down. The kids got very, very quiet. I didn't see fear in these children; it was, "Let's get this day started. This is what we are supposed to do, calm down, get quiet." They had an older child with them so they felt very secure and they just went to stay at the classes. I thought, "Gee, that's lovely."
>   Wherever you went in that school you saw happy children, whatever they were doing. They were all doing different things; they were interested. They were happy, they were relaxed, and they were excited about learning. When you saw the teachers, you saw

that same excitement, that joy. It was just perfect, that's how I felt
about it. . . .

At 3:00, when it was time to leave, the girls did not want to go.
I saw a lot of children staying around after school; no one was that
anxious to leave. Finally they kind of winded out of there. On our
way to the bus stop, the girls were just elated. They kept on and on
about the day. I said, "All right, if we can get you in, that's where
you go."

Once parents had chosen to send their children to CPE, the school
staff, and Director Deborah Meier in particular, spent a lot of time
and energy explaining CPE's theories of teaching and learning to parents
through weekly mimeographed newsletters, formal Parent Teacher
Association meetings, extended letters that served as report cards, and
individual parent–teacher conferences. When parents like Alice Douglass
discussed these formal communications channels, they were usually
positive.

As a matter of fact, the parent–teacher meetings were very good,
because they knew the kids very well. They used to tell you things
you would know as a parent; they weren't just giving a report, they
knew things that only a parent or someone that's around them
constantly would pick up on. They were very much into each
child's personality, and their needs. They were good at that; that
was important.

Mrs. Cartwright, who had some anxiety about whether her children
were being prepared for the competitive junior high schools she wanted
them to attend, also commented that CPE's reports on students' progress
helped her to understand what her children were really learning.

The reports on what the students were doing used to be handwrit-
ten, two pages on each student. Where are you going to find
teachers that are going to sit down and take that kind of time for
each student? That's better than looking at a grade, "A," "B," "C,"
or "needs improvement." I knew what my kids were doing.

Clearly, the fact that parents were impressed by their school visits to
CPE reflected the idea that they shared some of the school's values. One
thing Jomo Douglass's mother shared with CPE II was a belief that children should be brought up to be comfortable with people from a variety

of cultures and ethnic backgrounds. Mrs. Douglass grew up in Harlem, pre-dominantly among Blacks, and feels that

> I didn't miss out on anything, even though I didn't go to a mixed school, because we grew up around different nationalities. But the way things are now, with them growing up in this society, I think they should learn at an early age about all the different cultures that they're surrounded with. I figured in that sense [CPE II] was a great setting for them.

Jasmine Stevens's grandmother felt the same. A new school had recently been built across the street from where her family lived in Central Harlem, but Mrs. Stevens "didn't want her to go to the school there," even though the school building was certainly in better shape than the edifice that housed CPE. The reason: "I just wanted her to go to a mixed school." I asked Mrs. Stevens why this was important, in view of the fact that her daughter had had a bad experience in a newly integrated high school 20 years earlier.

> Well, I wanted [Jasmine] to learn both cultures. I didn't want her to stay at just one level and where one side of the world was living. Move around and just see what each culture was. That's the way, I felt, she would learn more.

"You didn't worry that she would have a bad experience going to schools run by Whites, as you did and your daughter did?" I asked. Mrs. Stevens answered:

> Well it's much better now than it was. I figured now that the world is a little more civilized, although racism is there. . . . I loved the school. I wish they had those schools when I was growing up, because the children have a sense of freedom, they can move around. When we were going to school, it was so much different. You had to sit there like a stiff all day long until recess. It was kind of hard, sitting there. You get bored.

Sabelle Cooper's family was sympathetic to Black nationalist currents in Harlem in the 1960s and 1970s, so CPE's integrated student body was not a factor in Mrs. Cooper's decision to send her daughters there. But the fact that CPE created an environment different from that of the crime-ridden neighborhood surrounding Martin Luther King Towers was a plus.

The kids were taken away from the ghetto and isolated from what's really happening for a few hours a day. That's what I liked about it. They were treated different from the nonsense that's going on in the regular average public school.

Nevertheless, parents reported that the warm personal relationships that developed between the parents and the CPE staff were most important in increasing their enthusiasm for the school. Like Mrs. Baker, Mrs. Pittman sent her daughters Tina and Vicki from West Harlem to CPE because after her divorce she found the Champ Montessori school too expensive. Once her daughters were at CPE, their sadness about leaving Champ disappeared.

A friend of a friend told me about this alternative education which I didn't know anything about. I made an appointment to see Debbie Meier and I took a tour of the school. I saw a lot of things happening that I enjoyed. . . . I liked the intimacy, the fact that the students knew the teacher, because that teacher was with them for a long period of time.

And there was a close relationship between the parent and the educator. We were on a first-name basis. We had their numbers, in case something went wrong and we needed to talk to them. There was a lot of personalized attention. It was a small school, a small environment. The students became very acquainted with each other. It was like an extended surrogate family, as I saw it. It was quite beneficial for my children at the time.

Mrs. Baker adds that the bonds teachers formed with parents helped cement the parents' support for the school.

There were some moments when I was having problems because of the divorce. I didn't have to talk about [it] in words, but there was support at CPE. I remember one particular teacher was having some problems also, and I went there one day for a meeting, and the teacher walked up to me and just talked, maybe 10, 15 minutes about the problems that they were going through, and it was all right, it was good. The support was there.

So I knew that whenever I had a problem, if there was something I wanted to talk about, I could do that. That's not the norm of what we think happens in schools; we don't think in terms of teachers and parents being able to talk that closely. In fact, we probably think that they shouldn't; we say that's not professional.

The teachers are just caring, very considerate people and when someone needed something, they responded. I think that they aren't even aware they are putting in special effort. Once a child sees that you respond to that need, the child feels comfortable to come back again and so it just continues.

Johnetta fell once and they had to rush her to the hospital. Debbie and Russ got her to the hospital before I got there, Columbia Hospital, and when I got there, Johnetta was being examined. I saw the look on Russ's face. He was in such pain and such fear. Immediately the nurses started assuring me it was just a very mild concussion and she should be fine in a couple of hours. And Russ and Debbie, they were so hurt, they felt so responsible, but it was an accident, it was an accident. I remember that night, Johnetta had to spend the night in hospital and they kept asking me, "Please, when you get home, call." I called to let them know she was okay, and they were so relieved. They were there; it was an accident but they didn't say, "This is not my responsibility."

Mrs. Douglass, whose son and daughter both attended CPE II, points out that the cause-and-effect relationship worked the other way too; the positive teacher–parent relations deepened the students' trust of their teachers and school.

The children have a different respect for their teachers and their parents when they see that you're friendly with your teacher, and you can sit down and talk and not debate and argue. The children are entitled to express their opinion, which I told them to. It took a while but they did talk about the things that they didn't like, and the next day, they went in and nothing was held against them. They felt comfortable about that.

So it was like a family unit. If I disagreed with something the teacher did, I gave her that respect and I spoke to her, not in front of my son, but I felt confident to say, "I don't like the way you did this." And then everything was fine. Nothing would be held against my kids. I think that's important in a school.

PARENT PARTICIPATION IN SCHOOL ACTIVITIES

Although most of the parents worked full time, there was an unusually high level of parent participation in school affairs. Betty Sherman and Marjorie Wilson were two leaders in the organization of parents in support of school fund-raising and lobbying efforts.

Before Betty Sherman came to CPE, she had been active in Harlem's civil rights movement and in West Harlem Democratic Party clubs. At CPE she shared her organizational expertise with the school.

When I first became a Parent Association co-chairperson, our first fund-raising event was in February. The day before our bazaar, it snowed. We were all biting our fingernails, wondering, "Is it going to work?" The day of the bazaar, it wasn't a question of the few and faithful doing the work. We had people to cover all the tables; we had games; we had clothes; we had food. The parents all worked so well with Jean Rojas and me. I was the outside person; she was the inside person. It was nothing to call up one of the parents and say, "I need to get the hot dogs picked up from some place." They'd say, "What time?" . . . The parents were absolutely terrific. We all did what we could. Somebody was working at a place where she had access to a couple of reams of paper; another person could run stuff off; this one had access to a telephone. Mr. DeSilver gave CPE the first answering machine that it had. We could not give CPE a lot of time but we just were able to plug in a little bit here and there to make it really work.

For Mrs. Wilson, who had organized neighbors to protest local real estate policies, participation in CPE was "thrilling."

I was always thrilled with those get-togethers at that school. They had a lot of potluck suppers and fund-raising events that really did bring us together. A lot of people from a lot of different back- grounds, to make the children have greater opportunities, strengthen their lives. I don't think you could send your kid to a school like that and not be involved because it's such a needy school.

We had to go to the community school district office many times. Debbie never called up to say, "I need you to go to the district office." But what she did do was she sent out a newsletter once a week. It would say, "There's a meeting coming up and we're going to leave the school at such and such a time." Those of us who could make it would show up.

Debbie was writing the newsletter every week. She was typing it herself. She may have been standing at the [Xerox] machine, cranking it out. So we said, "Well, what do you want, Debbie?" She said, she really would like a secretary. So we went up there to the district office and we made our demands known. She did get a secretary.

Every meeting at the district office started out with, "No, no, no, no," because they only had so much money to go around. . . . Mostly we dealt right with the superintendent. Of course, he was always too busy but then after we got talking and making our demands known and manipulating and all this stuff that you do in these meetings, he made time for us; he did. We had to play head games to get done what we needed to do. I had to cry and somebody else had to be angry; but we got through; we got the funding, or the extra space we needed in the school building.

Not every single parent, but those of us who could go, would go. We were all mixed and from different backgrounds, racially mixed and economically mixed, educationally mixed. We just knew that that was what we had to do that day, so we did it.

Parent participation was not limited to lobbying the district office for additional resources. Mrs. Wilson herself was inspired to take on several projects to improve school life.

We had to get the windows fixed and the garbage collected. . . . And we had to get on the super to sweep the play yard; he was talking on the phone, I don't know to who, but anyway, he did come along. And then we had to get some things painted. I must say, he did respond under pressure.

Also I had to get the lunchroom staff to be more receptive to the fact that you were trying to serve family style. Would they please serve it that way, rather than on individual trays. And go over the menu to see if we could get healthier food. I was really interested in that for a while, because I felt that my son Matthew had a lot of food sensitivities. I felt that the school diet was really contributing to the problem. I couldn't see why we had to buy food from Chicago and have it shipped frozen, when it might sit someplace and thaw and be refrozen. And then when the kitchen staff opened it, it was moldy. I couldn't see why our kids had to have that kind of food. I couldn't see why, when you would open the can, there was an inch of fat on the top. I didn't want the children to have that . . . that was one of my projects.

What made us so wonderful is the fact all of us were working. We all had to make money to support our lives, but that didn't stop us from putting the energy into the school and making the best life that we could for our kids. I always appreciated that about the parents; we were all so hardworking. There weren't any among us that weren't committed to this whole educational project. It was just thrilling to share it because whatever differences there were in our backgrounds or our life experiences, they didn't detract or complicate our coming together to make this school work.

Debbie was wonderful because she brought all this out in us. It was her vision and her communication with all of us that really brought us to a level that would not have happened otherwise.

In addition to participating in projects to support the school, some parents involved themselves in classroom activities. Ray Johnson, Lola's father, was a policeman often assigned to security duty at Yankee Stadium when the Yankees had home games. Not only did he obtain half-price tickets for CPE students, but he accompanied CPE classes to the ballpark on occasion. Mrs. Blake worked during the day, but went ice skating and roller skating with her daughters' classes whenever she could.

Whatever the children did, the parents were welcome to participate. I had a nice time, and I liked going to the school, participating in potluck suppers, and all the ethnic things they did, parades they would do, concerts they played.

CPE'S IMPACT ON PARENTS

Perhaps one of the more unique aspects of the CPE family was that the school wasn't a learning experience just for students, but for their parents as well. Mrs. Johnson, who teaches at a different East Harlem school, asserts:

I learned a lot as a parent there. Because Lola was such a monster, I was always very quick to whack her over the head. . . . Whenever there was any trouble, I was quick to yell, "Lola, what did you do now?" Debbie and Russ said, "Slow down, back down; listen first and don't be so quick to judge her." And that was a lifelong lesson. My role became one of support as opposed to constantly saying, "It's your fault, what did you do?" I'd have to listen and say, "Share with me, so that if I have to go in and defend you, I know what really went down." So Lola became pretty honest that way.

Mrs. Powers also credited CPE with contributing to her parenting skills.

It broadened me. It taught me a lot about how to be a better parent. It made me feel that you're not out there by yourself; life goes on and the school was out there to help you. For instance, if one of the children were having a problem, the teacher and I and the child would get together and we would talk it out. They would give us suggestions on how to deal with those problems, how to keep them in focus.

Similarly, Mrs. Wilson agreed that involvement at CPE was a formative experience in her own growth.

Because of my experience being a parent [at CPE], I really did learn to think about certain things that I wouldn't have thought about otherwise. I personally grew, and I think other parents did as well. We were encouraged [by Debbie] to look at education in a way that we hadn't looked at it before, a way that was other than, "Sit down and fold your hands," a way that was other than, "Be prepared to go work in a factory."

I guess you find out who you are too. The more you participate in the [school] community, the more you find out who you are. You don't have to be who you're not. You can be who you are. You can either accept it or not, the same as you would accept other people.

[The parents] were rich; they had so much spirit; they were so positive. Okay, we all griped once in a while, but generally we bought the dream, and were willing to work for it; the dream of letting the children be who they were and growing up not being afraid of children who were from different backgrounds and different life experiences.

While CPE began as an effort to empower teachers to plan and organize their students' education, it evolved into a school designed to encourage parent participation in educational decision making. As parents helped in school-building projects, as they joined in on classroom activities, as they became partners in conflict resolution, they developed a sense of involvement that encouraged them to make their own suggestions for improvement.

For example, by the time her daughter Jeanetta was nearing graduation, Mrs. Cartwright thought homework assignments could be handled differently.

I mentioned to Russ that I felt that Alice and Bruce should be allowed to give the sixth graders homework on a daily basis, instead of having reports to do every other week. This would prepare them to go to the traditional junior high schools. . . . That was just about my only criticism.

Dori Prince remembers her mother getting involved in a similar fashion at CPE II.

> Initially, my mother thought, "What have I done? My daughter is in this place and she's not learning anything." But then after a while she realized that she had to take part also and just try and help and give her input. I went to the parent–teacher conferences. I remember my teacher David saying he was really impressed with the books I was reading. He told my mother that CPE encourages that parents do things with their children at home and help them. So I think my mother liked that. She was really impressed that this is what they wanted you to do. Also I think she liked that because it helps the parent become more involved in their child's learning rather than the child going and the teacher takes care of everything. I think the teachers responded well to my mother. I remember David pushing me, and saying, "Your mother would like that you read more, so do your reading during reading time."

Mrs. Douglass went even further in describing how CPE II valued parents' input.

> The teachers at CPE make you feel that you're a part of their decision making; they don't shun you. You feel that what you say and what you do there is important, where the other schools are so big and there are so many parents with different ideas who want different things, it's conflicting. We all basically wanted the same, so we could work together. They made you feel like you were a part of their decision making; that's important to the parent as well as the child.

CONCLUSION

The alliance between the parents of CPE students and the school's staff was a key ingredient in the graduates' outstanding record. Parents were so enthusiastic about the new school and its progressive philosophy that their children quickly learned that their family and school were of one mind not only about the importance of learning, but about what children had to do to learn.

The high degree of parental support expressed for Central Park East surprised me, because my 1987 study had alerted me to parents' anxiety that their children would not be prepared to succeed in traditional secondary schools and colleges.

It may be that parents are currently more positive about CPE than they were when their children attended the school, because they've seen their children continue to do well. What's more, anxieties and reservations they had about CPE's child-centered approach may be forgotten retrospectively or dimmed in memory, whereas those things they always liked about the school may be all that's remembered.

In all honesty, another possibility for this disparity may be that I partially misunderstood parental reactions to CPE in my historical study. In hindsight, I realize that when I wrote that work, I made three assumptions about the parents' attitudes: first, that parents were influenced by the dominant society's emphasis on traditional educational approaches; second, that parents used their own school experiences as criteria in evaluating their children's; and third, that "many of the black and Hispanic working class parents had attitudes about authority and discipline that differ sharply from those of CPE's staff" (Bensman, 1987, p. 38).

After interviewing about 20 parents (and grandparents) who sent their children to CPE, I now think that all three assumptions in the preceding paragraph are questionable. In conclusion, then, I'd like to turn to the story of Mrs. Elsie Douglass, a licensed nurse who lives in the Health Care Workers' Union cooperative apartment development on 110th Street and First Avenue, as it illustrates the fallacy in all three of my assumptions.

Mrs. Douglass was not interested in finding a school like the one she had attended for the two children she raised by herself. She grew up in Harlem, on 129th Street and Fifth Avenue, born of parents who left South Carolina to make a better life in New York City.

It was important to Elsie's mother

> that we get our education, try to do the best we could, whatever our potential was, but that was it. She didn't push it, but she made sure that we had done our homework, that we were in school; she wasn't that active in school activities because she was so busy working, trying to care for the kids.

Looking back, Elsie thinks she wasn't

> challenged enough in school. My mother didn't research the school I went to. I went to school, I did what I had to do, and that was it. We did well in school, so I guess there was no reason for my mother

to really look into anything other than that, because that was accepted. I feel that I could have done much better had I had the opportunities.

When Mrs. Douglass's oldest child, Jomo, was of school age, she remembers:

I searched out schools. Things are different now. You can demand and there are more programs to get involved in. I wanted to do things with my kids that my mother didn't do with me, not for lack of her knowing, it's just that the opportunities weren't there, so any opportunity that I saw that would enrich the children, I wanted them to be involved in. I wanted to put him where the majority of the parents wanted the same thing for their children, not just to put them in school to say they were in school. I wanted a place where I could voice my opinion and where he could express himself as well. I wanted to put him in a setting where he would do his best, whether it be private or public school, so I sorted out different schools, where I thought he would do well.

Mrs. Douglass's drive to find the best school for her children also suggests that she was not a passive recipient of the dominant society's ideas about education. In part, Elsie chose CPE for Jomo because he

was getting bored. I needed a different concept, some change that would keep him interested in what he was doing, besides just the paperwork. He was still a kid, but I wanted him to grow socially as well as the intellect. At CPE, he was getting both of them growing up. And the mixture of different races. . . . The world that he's going to grow into, I want him to learn from each culture.

While Mrs. Douglass was uncomfortable with some aspects of CPE's culture at first, over time she discovered that she and the school shared many values.

It took a while for me to adjust with them calling the teachers by their first names, because I was brought up to address all adults "Mr." and "Mrs." But the children were comfortable with it. And some kids have pet names. The teachers chose to call the child by the name they would like to be called by. It was just like a family setting and I really liked that part. And I liked that they stayed with the same teacher for 2 years. The most important thing was that the kids were happy there. They were both somewhat quiet and after 2 or 3 years, I saw them opening up and being more confident with themselves. The social activities that they had in school and outside of school, I think they were beneficial to them. I feel that it's important to feel as comfortable in school as you would at home and around family. And that's how I felt, and that's how the kids felt, more or less.

Yet, while Mrs. Douglass eventually discovered that she shared many of CPE's values and beliefs about how children learn, she retained some skepticism about how CPE was preparing her children for future academic demands.

CPE brought him out of his shell, to be more of an intellect; he could express himself better. It was just a child developing and being able to deal the best that he could with things as they came along. I was impressed with that. But it took me a while to [adjust to] not having As and Bs. . . . I sent Jomo to Wagner Junior High School, which is back to the old traditional, structured school, because society says tests are important. So although I believe in what CPE wanted to do, it wasn't helping him in the sense he had to learn how to take tests and to do well on a standardized test. I think the confidence that he got from CPE helped him in going back to the structured school.

Mrs. Douglass reminds us that parents chose CPE not only because they sought an alternative to their neighborhood schools, but because they shared many of its values—caring, respect for others, expressiveness, creativity, racial tolerance. While CPE's learner-centered approach to teaching and learning was unfamiliar to most parents, they grew to trust the school as a whole because they liked the way teachers interacted with their children, and because they themselves formed positive relationships with CPE staff. At family conferences, parents learned how well the teachers understood their children; the elaborate reports on school progress reinforced parents' sense that they knew how and what their children were learning; Deborah Meier's weekly newsletters provided an explanation for the ways teachers organized classroom activities. In addition, parent participation in classroom and social activities, student performances and exhibitions, graduation exercises, fund raising, and lobbying on behalf of the school, helped cement teacher-parent bonds and gave parents a sense of involvement in the school.

In turn, parents found ways to participate in discussions about conflict resolution, curriculum, and homework policies. While CPE was established to realize the dream of teacher control and professionalism, parent involvement helped it transform into a school where a strong family–school relationship was recognized as essential to ensure students' continued success.

❧ 6 ❧

"And Then They Will Become Gifted": CPE Graduates Look to the Future

WHEN CPE GRADUATES describe their lives and their plans, they often refer, if only indirectly, to the values and lessons CPE passed on to them. They speak of intellectual curiosity and artistic expression, of self-reliance and cooperation, of social concern and ethical commitment, of critical thinking and the importance of education. Even when they criticize aspects of their elementary school experience, they demonstrate the ability and determination to make a better life for their children and for all our children. In the following excerpts from the interviews, six students reflect on how their time at CPE continues to influence them as young adults.

LOLA JOHNSON

Lola Johnson, a junior at SUNY–Oswego, believes that learning to challenge authority and think critically "in positive ways" at CPE has helped her in her premed major.

> Last year, I had a physics class where the professor solely went on your challenges. He had you read the chapters and do questions and he never answered a question. He always said, "What do you think the answer is and why do you think that that's the answer? Go home and think about it again. Read over the chapter. Do you still come up with that same answer?" Kids in the class could not deal with that way of learning. The other students said, "What, no tests, no exams, no finals?" I ended up getting an A in that class and it had to do with CPE. Because the other kids could not deal with that way of learning. . . . They said, "Why aren't you answering the question? The book says this; why don't you say it's so?" He would answer, "Books make mistakes. A person wrote this book. Why do

108

you think this is so?" I had so much fun in that class. This is his way of teaching and it's exactly how we were taught in elementary school. It was great.

I plan on going to med school, if I can afford it. I'm not sure what kind of medicine I'm going to practice. My chemistry teacher is trying to get me to go into chemical engineering now, but I really want to be a doctor. I wanted to be a surgeon, but I don't have any experience; I haven't done an internship yet. In the summer, there's an internship they're offering for juniors who are minorities, and you get to work somewhere. It's premed students, I think at Cornell. I'm going to look into that. Until I get some insight on different specializations, I really don't know.

I want to work in the city. I'll probably live in the city, or in Jersey, probably in the city. I like the city. I want to have an office out of a brownstone maybe, or my own office eventually, but I don't think I'm going to leave the city. I see myself working at 35, being a doctor and working in a hospital.

MARLA BAKER

Marla Baker, nearing graduation from Wesleyan College, is wrestling with the career choice she will soon face. CPE's impact on her own development looms large in her dreams about becoming an educator.

I'm thinking about getting two degrees, one in social studies and also counseling or social work. Some people have been saying that it's silly for me to get a degree. I don't really think I'll be a counselor or a social worker but it's been my other main thrust and I just really want to keep doing it, even if I may end up being a college professor or a teacher.

I think I'd enjoy doing both a great deal. Somebody lectured me last night actually: "Teachers don't make any money, Marla. What are you thinking?" I got so angry with him. I said, "Who are you? So you're in law school, so what? You've already made the decision that you want to make a lot of money. Let me make that decision."

I think it's wonderful to have people with any kind of under-dog background teaching because I think it's just an alternate side of something. Maybe one teacher could help. At CPE, where I visited yesterday, this girl asked, "Marla, what do you want to do?" and I said, "I think I want to be a teacher." She asked, "Are you going to teach African American history?" I said, "No, maybe women's history." She said, "I like that. I like that a lot." She started talking to me, "You wouldn't believe the sexism that goes on in this classroom." She started telling me about all the things that some of the boys in the class did.

Alternatives are important. They can only enrich a child's experience in school. Bruce was giving his students an alternative view of the history of civilization, yesterday. He said, "In European civilization they experienced the Dark Ages but in Africa they did not." I don't think that normally when students learn about civilization they get that lesson. So alternatives are so important, especially because the students may not be in CPE forever.

As a Black woman I've had a lot of teachers who just haven't said a word about Black women in history or Black women writers or politicians. Maybe my existence as a teacher who knows a lot about women's history is something that children can look toward, can ask questions to.

I've decided that I'm going to apply to grad school and I'm also going to apply for teaching internships. Part of me says "Take the time off and teach before you go in and get a degree to teach because you may decide that you don't want to do it. Maybe you should try it first," even though I feel that I have to be a teacher. My mother was saying that she thinks I'd be happier being a college professor and I thought that was true until this semester. She still may be right but right now this is something I really want to do. I want to teach in high schools.

STEPHANIE GONZALEZ

Stephanie Gonzalez, in customer relations at Xerox, and expecting a baby, believes that CPE has had a major impact on her maturation, an impact second only to that of her mother.

All those guys who went to [the zoned neighborhood school], they still stick together. All they do is hang out on the corner. They do bad things. And they have cars now. I look at myself and say, "I'm as old as he is, and he's driving a car." Not that I want to sell drugs; it's not that, but it's just so hard to believe that I know these people and they're doing this and they're doing that. I think, "I'm as young as you are and you have all these things." And they look like they're 30 years old. They look so old. I say to myself, "God." I wake up in the morning to go to work, and I don't see any of my friends, but come 5:00, I see them outside, hanging out on the corner and I say to myself, "They don't have to ride the train like me." I get so angry, and I think, "Why do you have to have it? Be like me. Be hardworking. Bust your chops like me." They just have that easy life. But I'm not saying I'm jealous or anything because I know it doesn't last. Look what happened to my friend on the corner. He got killed.

People always look at me as a role model. I want them to say to me, "Stephanie, how did you get this job? How did you know about computers? You work where? Oh you're so pretty." I want to be able to tell people, "You can do the same thing. You can look like me. You can be like me. You can have credit cards too. You can have a bank account. You can go and open up a bank account with $50. I'm not a millionaire." I always tell people, "You can be like me."

This friend of mine went to a computer training school, and then what happened? He packed up his stuff and he went to a boarding college. He wrote me a letter, saying "Thank you." He told me that when he went to class, all he would talk about is, "I know this girl; her name is Stephanie. She knows about this. She knows about that." He wrote me he was glad he was finally proving he could make it at college. So I wrote him back and I said, "You don't have to prove anything to anybody. Prove it to yourself." Because I couldn't go away to college. To this day, if I can have this baby and be in my house and also go to school, I will do it. If I had a choice to work or go back to school, I would go to school.

To tell you the truth, I don't really know the future. I always see myself as a single woman, so I do my thing now because I know in the future I'm going to be single woman. I'll stick to my job. I'll try to get as much education as I can. Sometimes I just read on my own, like about my pregnancy. I'm reading three books at the same time. It drives me crazy, yes, but, in a way, I have to educate myself. When I talk to my doctor, he says, "You're going a little ahead." It's only because I read.

I would like to go to college. I see myself like that. I really do. I'm in computers now and I'm a little secretary. I don't see myself like that in the future. Either I get a promotion in that same job and still go to school or I'll go into a different field.

I'm a secretary in sales; we handle the customers at the same time as we're doing our work, so it's kind of rough. You have these irate customers that come up with the craziest things. They'll say,

"I'm going to throw my machine out the window." They even curse
you out. And all you can do is either put the phone down or just
wish you were home. So far so good; everything's been okay, when
it comes to the job. . . .

[To train people, the company will] send them to a place called
Leesburg where they learn about customer relations. I say to myself,
"I'm not going to be on this floor for long." I want to get into
systems, the computer itself, not a sales rep. The sales reps are okay
but I'm really into the system. I'm more into service than sales.

I trained myself on the computer. At my old job, we had Xerox
equipment, and they put me on the machines. I had no idea about
this machine, so I had to learn on my own. . . . When it came to
troubleshooting the machine, I wouldn't even have to call the hotline.
My machine crashed so much that I'd reboot the machine all by
myself, by reading the manual and by putting in the diagnostics.

When it came to my job interview for Xerox, I told them I knew
how to do that, and I understood the tables and graphics and pie
charts too. They said to me, "You're crazy, you know all about
this?" It was just reading the books, that's all. They looked at it like
it's so hard, but it's just step by step. It tells you, "Insert this; take
out this."

[The education I got at CPE helped me to do that.] Because
anybody from [the neighborhood school] can learn about a computer, but, the way I was raised, with my mother and [CPE], it
helped a lot. We weren't the type of children that would come home
and say, "We had a fight." So my mother always looked at it like
the school is what always kept us going; we always looked forward
to going. We didn't say, "Mommy, I don't want to go to school
tomorrow." It was more like, "Mommy, I want to go to school
because we are going ice skating." So it came to a point, my mother
wouldn't even ask for my report card; she would not ask me for it
because she would always see me doing my homework. And after
all this, she always kept me organized. I guess to this day, that
helped me a lot because we went by a list: Monday do this; Tuesday
do this. Everything was in sequence so I was always brought up
like, "You do things like this, things like that." CPE did have a lot to
do with it, it did.

This incident that just happened, the shooting of my boyfriend's
cousin, it's really driving everybody crazy. Everybody just wants to
pack up and leave. I don't want to make it sound like I'm running
from my problems, but I think that it's just going to really make me
happier for the sake of my baby. It is.

I don't think living around here will work, I really don't. I think it's bad. As for my family, I will miss them. Yes I will. But if that's what's going to make me happy, I'm going.

The shooting of his cousin messed up my boyfriend's mind. Not that he was really close to him, it's just that it's happening to everybody. This block was such a community; everybody was so nice; everybody was together. All of sudden, everyone is just going into their houses, closing the doors. Nobody wants to be outside. He even tells me, "I wish you didn't have to walk your dog." I was telling him that this will always be my block, no matter what happens. I will always want to go there.

What I'm doing right now is I'm looking for a place to live, which is very, very, very hard. I don't want to live around here, but then I don't want to leave my mother. She was telling me yesterday, "If you want to leave, you can leave, as long as I know you're okay." What bothers me is that I do want to keep working. I will work until I can't work any more. But, when it comes to a babysitter, that's the only thing that's going to stop me, because if I move far away, I won't know anybody to babysit my kid.

I refuse to go on welfare. That's one thing that I cannot see myself doing. My mother did it. I'm learning from my mother, but like I told you about me being the single parent, I'm not having problems with my boyfriend, I'm just a person who likes to antici-pate. I want to feel that if my husband wants to leave my house, he can go and I can say to myself, "I did what I had to do; I have my job and I have a roof over my head." I don't want to be like my friends here: "My husband left and I have go on welfare; I'm back with my mother. I'm in the shelter. I'm in the home." I would never want to see myself like that.

But it's very rare that you see anybody succeeding around here, except for this side of the block, you see the brownstones. These are people that really don't have kids, and have their life straight or are retired. They just come out of work and go home. Their kids are not playing.

The other side of the street, it's like East Germany and West Germany. I say to myself, "It shouldn't be like that." I think every-body should be together but, unfortunately, it's not.

I asked my bosses at Xerox if they had [an operation] out in Baltimore because I just don't want to be out of a job either, and they do. So I could transfer. If that was to work, I couldn't be happier.

When it comes to marriage, my boyfriend told me, "Look, I'd like to get married." Not that he proposed to me on his knees, but he said, "I have an idea." He surprised me and I even asked him, "Are you drunk?" He tells me, "No, I'm dead serious." I ask him why, and he says, "Because you always told me the day that you have a baby you want to be married." I said, "That was my goal, it really was. But things don't happen the way that I planned to. I just don't want you to think it's an obligation, just because I'm having a kid, we have to marry. I don't. I don't think that's right. I don't want you to feel, 'I have to do it.'" I don't want to feel like I'm putting weight on his back. If he wants to, he can, if not, what can I say? It's just a thing that happened.

For being a single woman, my mother's doing a great job. That's why I look at myself and I say, "The day I have to be a single mother, I don't think I'll have any problem." You have the misery and you have the heartbreak, of course; everybody will go through that, but when it comes to responsibility and just bringing up a kid, I will just bring up my kid the way my mother brought me up, just like that, no better, no worse.

JIMMY O'ROURKE

Jimmy O'Rourke, a senior at Allegheny College in Ohio, is committed to social reform, a commitment that he can trace back both to his father and to his education at CPE.

My dreams are really up in the air right now. I'd like to teach. I love little kids, and if I were to teach, I'm sure it would be in the city someplace. What this country needs more than anything is education for people at a very young age and not just academic education but social education.

I also have an interest in writing, and I have an interest in film. Those are two things my dad's doing right now, but I also have an interest in going back to where I came from and doing something to correct a wrong I see, not in the community itself but in what's being done to the community—find some kind of cause to fight for.

In a lot of ways I feel this is a hypocritical, corrupted kind of society. A lot of that is due to bigotry and tendencies to cut people out because of the color of their skin. I just can't watch that for too long, I can't see that happening, I can't get too close to it and put up with it. A lot of my friends at school don't even think about it, so at this point in my life, it's hard to say how committed I am to that, or how much of my life I'm going to dedicate to that because it's a weird world I'm living in now.

I live with a lot of White people from the suburbs whose goal in life is to make a lot of money and have a nice house. That's not the way I've been brought up and I just wouldn't feel happy that way. I think I'll be heading toward graduate school, for sure. I've just declared religious studies as my minor. Taking this "Black religion, Black radicalism" course is really giving me a new view on religion because I never really believed in God. I never really understood why people could put so much faith in something they really have no real data about. I've just seen what society can do to people and why they could have so much faith. It's this whole learning process about people and what makes people tick. I think that's what I've learned and I think I'm going to want to teach that to other people or to help people understand it.

VALERIE SANCHEZ

Valerie Sanchez, a junior at the University of Puerto Rico in Rio Piedras, is very involved in her family's church. She has adjusted successfully to life in Puerto Rico, but she wants to return to New York to put what she learned at CPE into practice, helping immigrant children.

I'm studying to be an English teacher, to teach English as a second language. I'm in my second year. In 2 years I will have my bachelors degree. Once I get my bachelors degree I'll have to stay in Puerto Rico because I want to get my masters. But once I have my masters I would like to go back to New York, or Florida, and get a job teaching English. They are two states that have a lot of Hispanics, have bilingual programs.

I want to teach English as a second language. Since I like dealing with kids, I would teach English on an elementary level. I've always wanted to be a teacher. I teach here at church. I learn as much from the children as they learn from me. They see things in their own way, which shocks me at first but I say, "It has logic; it's something I have to accept." They surprise me in many ways. Some of the things they come up with, although it's concerning spiritual things, it's still an everyday life situation. I love giving the class.

I like Puerto Rico, and I want to get my masters here. I like the university where I'm studying. It's a good university here in P.R. and

I'm proud of studying there. I want to teach English, here, to see what it's like but I also feel that desire to teach English in the States.

Education in New York isn't like education here. I want to have that experience of teaching in the state where I grew up. I will be the teacher, not the student. I would like an open class setting like in CPE, that type of relationship between students and teacher. Although even if I do teach in a normal classroom, I would still change that type of relationship between me and the students. I would want the students, for example, to call me by my first name. I wouldn't want the seats in a row. I would try to make the best of the classroom setting. If I could, I would make a circle with the seats and try and get that relationship between student and teacher as I had in CPE. I don't know how many changes I could make to the classroom to get away as much as I could from that ordinary look, but if I did have to teach in an ordinary classroom, I would try as much as I could to make it so that they would experience what I did in CPE.

JASMINE STEVENS

Jasmine Stevens, in her description of the kind of school she wants to teach in, adopts a multicultural position that did not exist in CPE's early years, when Jasmine studied there. Yet Jasmine still feels CPE's vision is very close to her own, and when she describes the difference between what she believes in and what she learned as a child, the very act of her reflecting critically and coming to a new pedagogical position, one that shares the humanist values of CPE, is perhaps the best affirmation a school like CPE could hope for.

This next semester will be the first time I'm taking a whole bunch of education courses, so I will really get the gist of how I like going to college then. The courses that I'm taking now, the math courses and sociology, the reading and writing courses, are similar to high school. They are just an extension of what they taught you there. I liked going to high school, so of course I'm going to like these courses now. But this semester I'm going to take four education courses so I'll get to finally realize what college is all about. I'm really working toward my education degree and I'll get it. I'll probably be doing student teaching next year.

I'm going to start student teaching a year from this spring. I want to teach younger children, but my boyfriend says it's best to be able to work in a college or something like that. You have to work your way up, so I don't know if I'm going to go right from school into a school teaching. I want to get a masters degree.

[I want to teach in a school like] Central Park East. I told my teacher that too. Also, the Early Childhood Learning Center, it's a group of schools run by Moslems, more or less Moslems. It's similar to Catholic schools in a sense. It's a Moslem school and it was on television. This video show called *Video Box* did a program about this school, the Early Childhood Learning Center. I liked it a lot because I have a problem with the way history is usually taught. I hate it. I think they teach false history, because you're taught things like Christopher Columbus discovered America and he didn't. Those kind of things bother me. Why do they teach those type of things? That Moslem school, they teach about how Africans are part of the making of this country. It's not false teachings. They have people who are White as well as Black proving that these things really happened, that all of the gold and the oil and all the fruits and vegetables that we've got here came from Africa. Those are the kind of things that I want my Black community to know about, to know that we didn't just come here as slaves but we had a great impact on America. I want my community to know that we are responsible for all the clothing we wear because we picked all the cotton. It wasn't just that we were slaves and that was it. We built this country to where it is, along with other people. Even though all these White people did a lot of things, we discovered the traffic light and we did all those things that I didn't learn about until I got out of high school.

Everyone knows about their culture except for us. You skim right over the Africans. It was just that they came here as slaves and then slavery was abolished and Abraham Lincoln abolished slavery. There's proof that Abraham Lincoln got a deal, where if he abolished slavery he could get something out of it; he didn't abolish slavery because he felt sorry for the slaves, he abolished slavery because someone said, "If you do this and we let Blacks vote, then they may help you stay where you are," so that's why he did it. Those are the kinds of things I think you need to know, as well as everything else that I learned. We've been left out a lot and the history department in these schools, they don't teach you.

[When I teach Black children,] I'll want to teach them about themselves. Because I think if you learn that you did a lot, it will cause you to want to help keep up what we've done so far. How many Black men are in jail? Those are the kind of things I hear a lot. There's too many negative things. There's this little boy, who I was talking to, who was saying that Black people created drugs, or something. He said that we're the only people that sell drugs, and we created it. He believed that if you were famous and you were Black you were on drugs. That bothered me. I had to explain to him . . . that Black people aren't the only people that sell and use drugs.

It's something wrong with the system. I think if you teach something, you should teach it in full and not halfway. You don't teach how to add and not teach how to subtract; you teach both of them. I've got by, but if knowing what George Washington did, and what Lincoln did and all these people did, is so important and they're humans just like me. . . . You're being left out. I didn't know I was being left out of all of this stuff until I got to a higher level. And then you find it out and you say, "how come I didn't learn it?"

We're going to be left here when all the people older than us are gone and we're going to have to create something to live by. And if we have such a negative view of ourselves, we can never reach for what we should be reaching for. Jesse Jackson told a lot of people that a Black person could even run for President. A lot of people didn't even know that. I'm sure younger people didn't even think that could exist. Just by him running, that taught a lot of people that that could be done. You're constantly reminded how negative you are and how negative your group is. I think it's up to us to teach our people, if no one else is going to teach us. I'm sure Jewish people know their history and where they come from. I know their history. They don't know my history. Why is that, when there might be more of us than there are of them?

I met this man named Jerome Bruner, and I told him all my ideas. He's responsible for a lot of curricula in the schools. I'm so glad that I got to meet him because I wanted to speak to someone that has experience in changing something out of the norm. He had a class learn all about Alaskans and Eskimos, a whole curriculum on it. That's the kind of thing I want to create, something that you don't learn every day that will help you in real life, just as well as calculus will. I told him my ideas and he took my name and address down and he said they were some good ideas.

I told him maybe when I graduate, I could come to him for ideas. I want to create a school. It's not really a school for the gifted; it's a school to create gifted. You take young children and put them in school, in a fun but learning environment at the same time, and then they will become gifted.

❧ 7 ❧

Creating a Learning Community

I ORGANIZED THIS STUDY to address the reservations expressed by people (myself included) skeptical that CPE's achievements really measured up to its reputation. At the beginning, I expected resistance to center around the graduates' school achievements. Could I really prove that CPE graduates did better than comparable graduates from other schools?

Even after I reached 117 of the 135 graduates and showed that more than 9 in 10 graduates had completed high school, and two-thirds had gone to college, critics were not convinced. They simply shifted grounds, claiming that CPE had achieved its sterling reputation by "creaming the pool" of East Harlem students. Again, I took this objection seriously by looking closely at the graduates' backgrounds, by examining the process by which they were selected, and by constructing the best comparison group I could. When I concluded that graduates of the Central Park East Elementary School achieved substantially higher rates of high school completion and college entrance than did the population selected for comparison—the total New York City public school population—I encountered new objections.

For example, when I brought my data to the attention of an education reporter for the *Wall Street Journal*, he dismissed them. CPE's success was not significant because it could not be duplicated elsewhere, he argued. CPE was an exceptional case that depended on the genius of its founder, Deborah Meier. This, however, is a circular argument. How do we know that Deborah Meier is a genius? Because she won a MacArthur "Genius" Award. Why did she win the award? Because her school was excellent. Why was her school excellent? Because she is a genius. . . .

By now it's clear to me that some critics of child-centered education can never be satisfied. In all likelihood, some of them will never accept the idea that "typical" students of color can achieve high rates of success because this conflicts with their views of the country's minority population. Others will not believe in CPE's achievement because to do so would raise questions about why so many other schools are failing children at risk.

Nevertheless, today there are millions of Americans committed to improving the quality of public education, and open—sometimes too open—to considering new approaches and re-examining old ones. In hopes of aiding their efforts, I will bring together what I understand to be the crucial ingredients in CPE's success. To do so, I will draw on the graduates' testimony. But as students cannot have an historical perspective about how an educational institution developed its strength, we need to look beyond their evidence to the organizational development of CPE over time. Looking at CPE's story through the lens of contemporary literature on organizational development, I argue that, in part, CPE achieved its success because it possessed significant, and replicable, organizational strengths that enabled it to develop, refine, and continuously improve its educational ideas and practices.

GRADUATES EXPLAIN THE SCHOOL'S SUCCESS

Graduates attributed their success to the fact that CPE taught them invaluable lessons. Inside and outside formal educational settings, they continued to carry with them the following lessons:

1. Learning is enjoyable.
2. They can trust their own judgment, experience, and artistic impulses.
3. They possess valuable strengths on which to build.
4. Asking others for help in solving problems and overcoming weaknesses brings support and yields successful solutions.
5. Working with, helping, and being helped by others yields power and satisfaction beyond what an individual can produce alone.
6. The world outside their homes and neighborhoods contains resources they can access and utilize.

Graduates not only achieved higher academic success rates in school than their counterparts in other New York City schools, but they testified that the school contributed as much to their emotional and social growth as to their academic development. Furthermore, the graduates described gains in the academic sphere as being inseparable from those in the emotional and social sphere; growth in one accompanied and was made possible by growth in the other. Over and over again, students told me that their teachers provided the support and encouragement they needed to discover an interest and develop a skill. As they developed and became recognized for a skill, their self-esteem improved and they took on greater academic challenges.

Essentially, students told me that I could not simply compare CPE with traditional schools if I wanted to explain graduates' high rates of academic achievement. Instead of considering CPE unique merely because of its curriculum and teaching practices, I should see it as a learning community where children could grow as human beings, in addition to growing as students. Products of this environment, the graduates not only achieved higher rates of high school completion and college entrance, but were also more likely to

1. Be critical in their approach to information
2. Ask "what is right" or "what should be" than to accept things as they are
3. Appreciate diverse cultures and incorporate elements from those cultures into their own ideas and expressions
4. Adopt their own solutions to problems rather than reproduce the solutions of authorities

In other words, graduates suggested CPE's effectiveness should be judged in terms of its own values, and not simply the individualistic and materialistic values that often are accepted as "the norm" in American society. As graduates talked about what they are doing now and what they hoped to do in the future, as they described their triumphs and setbacks, their hopes and dreams for themselves and their children, graduates testified that CPE's founders successfully passed on their legacy—a belief in the dignity of the individual and the value of cooperative effort; commitment to social equality and cultural diversity; and respect for the human spirit's creativity and the American citizen's communal responsibility.

CREATING PATHWAYS TO LEARNING

Why did graduates make such progress? Graduates described their learning experiences as long-term processes by which teachers helped them develop pathways to academic learning, starting from interests students brought from home or discovered in the classroom. To enable students to embark on their own pathways, teachers employed methods that allowed students to understand the points at which they were starting, what information they possessed, what assumptions they relied on, what things interested them, and what did not.

To create these pathways, CPE had to abandon a basic principle of American urban education: that all children are to be regarded as the same. Rather than succumb to what education historian Lois Weiner (1993) calls the schools' "systemic incapacity to accommodate differences," CPE teachers learned not only to build on differences but to make them a source of strength.

Doing so required teachers to listen carefully and respectfully to what children said and to observe their activity sympathetically, rather than constantly judging them against external standards. Teachers devised open-ended projects that allowed children to enter schoolwork from a variety of starting points, and to engage in multiple activities that developed skills and deepened and spawned new interests.

As always, academic learning was supported by CPE's emphasis on nurturing the emotional and social growth of the students. Through their interactions with students, members of the school staff demonstrated that they cared about students as human beings. Relationships in the CPE community were based on caring, respect, and mutual trust. Graduates drew strength from these relationships, maturing emotionally and socially in the process. Furthermore, CPE was able to bridge racial and cultural divides; the "integrationist" ethic of CPE's founders flourished in a world where integration as a social ideal was losing its luster.

In part, what made this nurturing environment possible was CPE's small size: Everyone in the school knew everyone else's name; teachers knew the parents not only of their own students, but of many other students; students knew each other's parents and sisters and brothers. When CPE attracted so many applicants that its small size was threatened, the school spawned a separate small school, CPE II, rather than relinquish its intimate character.

But small size alone did not make CPE an intimate community; the values and attitudes that the CPE staff brought to their job were equally important. Teachers treated students the way they wanted their own children to be treated in schools, as whole human beings needing affection and respect as well as guidance. Indeed, sometimes CPE students were the teachers' own children. Even when they weren't, though, teachers and students alike brought their families into the learning environment through school trips, school parties and celebrations, and informal gatherings.

Teachers were willing to involve themselves so fully in the school environment because CPE's culture supported and encouraged them to do so. In her relationships with her staff, Deborah Meier was open about her own needs and values, and expressed interest in each of the teachers as individuals. She talked to each teacher one-to-one, person-to-person; based on what she learned about her staff, she made elaborate efforts to accommodate each individual's personal needs; and she supported each member of the faculty to develop professionally, with school resources as well as personal encouragement and advice. In other words, Meier treated the staff much the same as they treated their students—with respect, courtesy, and compassion.

PROCESS OF CREATING A LEARNING COMMUNITY

When Meier first founded CPE, there was no set progressive education blueprint that staff members brought to the school. On the contrary, many of CPE's strategies and policies were adaptations to unforeseen situations. For example, when two teachers decided they needed to spend more time with their infant children, Meier accepted their proposal that they work half days as partners. When another teacher decided she wanted additional training, Meier let her leave the school, with an understanding that she could come back later. These kinds of decisions indicate that CPE became an organization possessing the same abilities it tried to inculcate in its own students—the ability to define problems, to seek help and expertise from others, and to continuously improve its practices and performance (see Heckscher & Donnellon, 1994; Raywid, 1985). CPE was an organization that learned how to learn.

Respect for Teacher Professionalism

Central to CPE's ability to continuously grow and improve was a basic respect for teachers' professional competence. At a time when most of American education was experiencing a "reform" that removed whatever control of curriculum teachers still retained and transferred it to central bureaucracies, CPE successfully forged a path toward teacher professionalism: Members of the staff defined critical issues, discussed them collectively and at length, and participated in devising solutions. Sometimes those solutions involved reaching out to external sources, as described in Chapter 2. Attending summer workshops and collaborating with educational consultants were only some of the many ways CPE teachers were willing to go outside their classrooms to develop new ways of better connecting with their students.

Since teachers believed themselves to be valued and respected, they contributed immense amounts of their time and energy to improving their teaching practice. This effort at continuous improvement was partly an individual matter; each teacher created his or her own curriculum, collected and provided necessary learning materials, and designed lively learning environments. But the effort at continuous improvement was also collective: At frequent and lengthy meetings of the instructional team, members of the staff voiced their problems, defined their concerns, identified their needs, and shared their individual techniques and solutions.

In the course of these meetings, teachers discovered that many problems they had thought to be beyond their control could be addressed strategically, by changing aspects of the learning environment. Problems that had once seemed to be a result of a teacher's individual inadequacies were discovered to be shared failures that new teaching techniques could overcome. What seemed like students' idiosyncrasies were actually responses to aspects of the school environment that could be changed. Likewise, what had seemed to be symptoms of family or community problems beyond the school's control could be remedied through collective action by school staff or by teacher–parent partnerships.

As participants discovered that they had the power to solve problems that they themselves defined as important, they found new energy and resources within themselves to contribute to devising new solutions. In the language of contemporary organizational studies, CPE became an "effective" organization (Heckscher & Donnellon, 1994; Howard, 1993).

Leadership and Support

Strong leadership by Deborah Meier facilitated CPE's development of openness to the outside world, teacher professionalism, and commitment to continuous improvement, but Meier's leadership style was itself the product of organizational learning. In the beginning, CPE had no leader; the school was established as a 1960s-style collective because the teachers feared "authoritarian leadership." As a response to unanticipated problems, Meier's role changed from that of first teacher among equals, to that of a leader responsible for providing support for teachers, for being their spokesperson, and for negotiating with the outside world.

In its first 2 years, CPE teachers had had small classes but no free time and no support. All teachers worked in the classroom, which meant that class size was small, and each teacher could select work materials, design a curriculum, and schedule the school day. While this gave everyone a feeling of freedom, it also produced great pressure as there was no one to provide backup for teachers on all the day-to-day problems that inevitably arise. Teachers had to deal with all the school's paperwork, as well as talk to parents, counsel troubled children, plan trips, and order supplies. And when a teacher had a problem with a student, or with a curriculum that didn't seem to work, no one was there to provide support and advice. (There wasn't even anyone to answer the phone.) What CPE teachers had hoped would give them the freedom to be great teachers had instead made them isolated, overextended, and overworked, even "irritable and sensitive," Meier concluded.

During the summer after CPE's second year, Meier realized that teacher autonomy from administrative interference and small class size were not sufficient principles for the operation of an effective school. Her new organizational plan created additional support for teachers, established a new role for the administration, encouraged more collaborative work among school staff, and eliminated staff overinvolvement in the details of school life.

Meier proposed a structure under which she would serve as director, charged not only with coordinating CPE's activities with the district office and with P.S. 171 (the building in which CPE was housed), but also with providing support for each classroom teacher. Meier's new role was to be an advisor or master teacher, a role more akin to an English headmistress than to a traditional principal. Meier comments: "I remembered what my experience with the Open Corridor programs in Districts 2 and 3 should have led me to earlier: A good staff needs someone to play an advisory role, to provide both stretch and support. Such a role is as important for competent and experienced ones. I myself had longed for such help during my last year of teaching."

In CPE's new organizational scheme, support for teachers went beyond the director's mentor role. In addition to assigning an aide to each cluster of classrooms, Meier assigned one aide to CPE's new office, to relieve the teaching staff of such administrative burdens as keeping attendance records, collecting breakfast money, filing lesson plans, and responding to a variety of Central Board requests for information on student performance and teaching practice. Furthermore, Meier was determined to provide teachers with normal preparation periods, a child-free lunch break, follow-up help in working with children who needed additional resources, and an end to so much obligatory meeting time after school hours.

In place of weekly meetings, CPE's staff developed a flexible mix of formal and informal gatherings where they could transact school business. The school's new schedule made informal collaborative time available by providing teachers with duty-free lunches and overlapping prep periods. Whole-school programs, such as movies and sings, made it possible for the staff to meet weekly during the workday to discuss organization problems; this gave teachers real control over the life of the school on an ongoing basis. Two to three times a month, the teachers also organized, chaired, and directed separate after-school meetings where the entire staff discussed such serious educational questions as how to work better with individual children, how to develop curriculum, and how to improve articulation between lower and upper grades.

Meier also arranged ways for teachers to visit each other's rooms, to observe classes at other schools, and to take part in professional activities outside CPE. To accomplish this, Meier sometimes had to take over a teacher's class for part of a day, or even a whole day. This gave her an opportunity to understand better the problems each teacher was facing, to know the students better, and to see for herself the strengths and weaknesses of the class. Getting into the classrooms also had the incidental function, Meier reports, "of reminding me how tough it is to teach, and how the best ideas in the world aren't always appropriate for a given class or teacher."

As important as the leadership of its first director, Deborah Meier, was in shaping CPE's culture, external support and leadership were equally essential. If Superintendent Anthony Alvarado had not "orchestrated diversity," in the East Harlem District, if he and his successor Carlos Medina, and his assistant Seymour Fliegel, had not exercised firm support of CPE when it experienced the opposition that arose inevitably during the school's formative years, CPE's story would have been a tale of promise unfulfilled, as are so many stories of educational innovation (see Heckscher & Donnellon, 1994; Raywid, 1985).

PATH TO EDUCATIONAL REFORM

Any discussion about how CPE's success can be replicated need not stop with dismay over the impossibility of duplicating Meier's genius; instead, those seeking the critical path to school effectiveness should start with an assessment of CPE's organizational strengths, in order to figure out how to create those strengths in different circumstances (when there is no Deborah Meier available).

If one reflects on CPE's strengths in an effort to chart a course to "create many CPEs," it becomes obvious that while support from administrative authority is essential, no reform effort can be imposed top-down. If small, child-centered schools are mandated from above, and designed according to blueprint, without enlisting the input and commitment of teachers and parents, the new schools will be unable to mobilize their participants' energies and knowledge, and will lack the capacity to "learn how to learn."

Nor can we expect that teachers trained to carry out the plans of educational authorities will be able to organize and participate in site-based management. After all, CPE's staff was drawn from a small group of teacher education and preparation institutions that stressed preparing teachers for child-centered education. If the United States decided to create "many CPEs," we would need to reform teacher education on a large scale and enhance teachers' professional development opportunities (Darling-Hammond & Goodwin, 1993).

Furthermore, attempts to replicate CPE within the context of central administrative systems designed to ensure curricular and pedagogical uniformity would likely become mired in endless struggles to gain case-by-case exceptions to the standard operating procedures—a handicap under which CPE I and CPE II long labored (Raywid, 1985). The search to circumvent or gain freedom from Central Board rules consumed countless hours of Deborah Meier's time and made organizational innovation a continuing headache.

Of course, explaining CPE's success and growing influence solely in terms of its organizational change sorely overlooks an essential component of CPE's success: its commitment to the well-being of all of its members, including their need not only for achievement and recognition, but also for emotional intimacy, for caring, love, and support. The way people at CPE cared for one another did not have clear limits: Relationships extended outside the classroom, after the school day, during vacation periods, and beyond graduation. Even after they've been away from CPE 20 years, graduates like Marla Baker and Lola Johnson return to their school year after year to maintain old relationships and keep in touch with new developments. Parents of graduates send their other children there, urge relatives and neighbors to enroll, and continue attending graduations and celebrations. Perhaps it would be better to call the school a "learning community" than a "learning organization."

In conclusion, this review of CPE's remarkable trajectory suggests that the challenge facing American society is not to discover a blueprint for reform; rather we must strengthen the networks of public and private institutions and community organizations that nurture our schools' efforts to develop essential capacities for learning, growth, and inspiring others.

Furthermore, we need to redefine our conception of education so that we embrace the importance of children's social and emotional development as well as their academic achievement. Redefining education in this way would have profound implications for the way schools are organized, for social and emotional development grows out of caring relationships, relationships between one whole human being and another. Schools that sustain and nourish such relationships today are rare and face many dangers; they will flourish and propagate only when there is a widespread social agreement that they are essential to the survival of our democracy.

Afterword

ONE LEGACY OF my teaching life at Central Park East is an immense and unmanageable collection of papers. Some of it is children's work, but most is mine. There are packets of written observations of individual children, narrative reports on children (our version of the traditional report card), school journals, children's writings, play scripts, homework assignments, lesson plans, curriculum plans, math worksheets, map-making exercises, notes of meetings, notes about notes, notes of observations, notes of Descriptive Reviews of children and their works, articles from scholarly journals and popular magazines, clippings from newspapers, copies of articles with titles like "Math Activities for the Open Classroom." The upper corner on some sheets has a scribbled note from Debbie: "Interesting," she writes, or "Has some good ideas!"

Papers spill out of ragged manila folders that are piled in untidy heaps on bookshelves; the overflow has been stuffed into file cabinets and plastic milk crates. Boxes and bundles take up too much space in my workroom and clutter up the attic. It takes forever to find something I actually want because I have no idea where anything *is*.

Without any clear purpose, I have been saving this stuff for 20 years, and now I'm stuck with it. Obviously, I can't just throw it away. I half believe that there is vital information about teaching and learning in those notes; and who knows when I'll need those math ideas, experiments with density, directions for making corn husk dolls, tips for writing radio plays? At least, that's the story I tell myself, but the real reason is complicated and difficult to express without sounding pretentious or maudlin. When I leaf through the children's work, or turn the pages in my old school journals, I find reading what's written there very hard to bear. My impulse is to shut the book, refold the bundle, pack up the papers and put it all away. It hurts to look; remembering makes me uneasy. So much of my adult life is in those pages, inextricably woven together with the school lives of children who became the "graduates" this book describes. So much time and thought, effort and anguish—mine *and* theirs; so much wondering and worrying; so much tracking and backtracking; so many unanswered, perhaps unanswerable, questions. They tumble around in my mind, still troubling after all these years. Some are about everyday teaching matters—what else can I do about fractions, punctuation, times tables, map symbols? Some are the large, haunting ones, the stuff of bad dreams: Did I do the right things? Did I teach them well? Are they prepared? Will they succeed?

Reader, they *did* succeed, well beyond even my grand hopes for them.

David Bensman documents that success, in this study of the graduates' lives, citing statistics that reflect high school graduation rates, college admissions, professional careers, work histories, marriages, new families. The figures dearer to my heart are not fully represented here. They reflect the newest, youngest members of our student body, the second generation of CPEers, the children of the children we taught.

More rewarding for their old teacher to read than stats and graphs are the recollections of the graduates. Having known them as children, I expect variety and liveliness in their stories. I know I'll hear distinctive voices and I'm not disappointed. But there is a common theme evident throughout. The graduates echo one another in acknowledging that their early schooling, at Central Park East School, *made a difference*. Some describe, in detail, the effect of their school experiences on their later lives. I love reading the stories even as I recognize that the testimony is biased. It is colored by nostalgia and sentiment, and the absence of other school experiences with which to compare their own.

The perspective that provides the needed balance, makes the contrasts clear, and defines what made us special is in the stories told by students who transferred to our school in the fourth, fifth, and sixth grades. Their recollections, set alongside my long-ago reflections and notes, let me see how some of those older children experienced this new, slightly weird school. They were surprised and delighted by our attentiveness, our readiness to listen to their ideas, complaints, questions. That sort of concern from teachers was a new experience for them. My journals are full of lists of appointments for meetings, notes of conversations with this child and that, questions they raised for me and worries about what to do next. Sometimes I consulted Debbie, sometimes other staff members. It was a comfort to be able to share my worries with others who often knew a youngster better than I did. During the school year, we did Descriptive Reviews of children who raised special concerns; in July, I took bundles of papers to the Prospect Summer Institute and worked on child studies. Children were at the center of our work. We taught them that, along with everything else.

Whenever I talk or write about Central Park East, I have a struggle with language. Should I use the singular or plural pronoun; present tense or past? Should the emphasis be on teacher-as-soloist or on the ensemble of very fine practitioners of which I am merely one member? Describing

Central Park East as it *was* implies that it is now something else and alters the sense of our school as a living institution where much current practice is continuous with the past, but also different in significant ways. It's a philosophical quandary as well as a linguistic one. So I mix past and present, singular and plural, hoping that my intentions are clear, although I'm never sure whether I have gotten it right.

Pronouns create another kind of difficulty. On the other hand, it seems natural to think and use *we* because that expresses our collective identity and reflects our vision of the school as a place where staff members shared in the education of one another as well as of the children. On the other hand, each of us prized the freedom and autonomy that the school conferred; we were insistently independent and very protective of the special relationships we worked so hard to establish with our own group of students. *My kids, my classroom* as personal territory was guarded with some tenacity, even though it necessitated a good bit of juggling to balance the role of soloist with that of ensemble member.

There were other complications. We wanted our school to be a community of learners and, not being sure what that meant, weren't sure how to go about achieving it. Our educational philosophy had its roots in several different sources. Without ever making the connections explicit, we thought of ourselves as following in the tradition of John Dewey and likeminded educational progressives at the Laboratory School. Many of us trained with Lillian Weber at the City College Workshop Center and were champions of Open Education. Others were introduced to the philosophy and practices of the British Infant Schools by Wendla Kernig and the staff at Community Resources Institute. Through training and inclination, we were fervent believers in communitarian ideals, but the *me* and *mine* thinking was equally powerful. Even at the best of times, balancing all the elements was not easy.

Although the classroom was the private, personal space into which each teacher and her or his group could retreat, it was impossible for any one of us to be the teacher in the "hermetically sealed classroom" that Sarason describes. For one thing, sharing was a way of life. Our classrooms required materials of all kinds, and someone else was likely to have the very thing you needed. Much of the stuff we used was junk materials and found objects, scavenged and collected by staff members or donated by parents. Some of the stash might be stored in my room, but it was recognized as common property and meant to be shared by everyone. We also "borrowed" pretty freely from one another since there was never enough of anything—Unifix cubes or guinea pig food or blue paint—to go around. Finally, there was an occasional need to "share" physical space: a quiet corner in someone else's room as a time-out spot for a youngster who was acting up, or places where older kids and their younger "reading buddies" could sit together to share books. All these interwoven needs made it difficult for one to withdraw to her classroom and shut away the rest of the school world. Inevitably, a sense of community grew from these informal comings and goings. Popping in to borrow a ball of twine meant spending a few minutes observing and catching glimpses of the work going on in a colleague's room; asking for help with a youngster or advice about curriculum invited reciprocity.

As a staff, we were great talkers. Early in the morning or at the end of the day were the likeliest times: Lunchtimes were hard because there was so much else to do besides sit and eat. More formally, we all attended a 2-hour weekly after-school staff meeting. The "school community" was a topic that came up frequently. We worried that the children did not have a strong sense of community because we didn't; that the boundaries between classrooms were quite firmly established and difficult to cross. We worried about issues of diversity and inclusivity, and how they affected children's relationships with one another and with adults. Periodically, we tried to carry out a common, school-wide curriculum, thinking it might serve to draw us together. We succeeded only once, I think, during the year of the *Treasures of Tutankhamen* exhibition at the Metropolitan Museum. What created a genuine sense of community were school-wide events that became CPE "traditions"—concerts, play performances, potluck suppers, family picnics that brought children, parents, and staff together several times a year.

Another way in which we were able to share work and children without invading or interfering with each other's personal boundaries or relationships with students, was through the use of the Prospect processes. We never did as many Descriptive Reviews as we planned, or followed through as diligently as we intended, but the use of the processes established a way of looking, seeing, and thinking about children and teaching practice that was grounded in observation, substituting shared thought for criticism, and recommendations from colleagues for mandates from the director.

The interplay of personal and communal needs created tensions, but also lent a sense of heightened intensity to our work. After a time, we found that a particular problem, identified in our in-house code as a particular teacher's "burning issue," needed to be resolved. Since there was no formula for doing any of this, solutions were improvised and often provisional, a let's-try-it-and-see-what-happens-because-we-don't-know-what-else-to-do approach. Some things remained fuzzy, unresolved, messy, and open, which left everyone a bit dissatisfied, but also left room for more improvisation.

There were issues we sidled up to gingerly, guided by a common, unspoken understanding of their destructive potential. When the issues were ones that could not be "managed" so quietly, staff meetings became tense, awkward, contentious. Some of us had a half-humorous, half-serious battle with Debbie about whether one could/should "teach" spelling. Another memory, still painful after all these years, is of a discussion among staff members about issues of race that led to accusations of favoritism in children's class assignments. Obviously, conflicts were not always resolved, or hurt feelings assuaged, but we managed to keep the most difficult issues inside their frames and avoided the great rifts that could have destroyed the school.

To some extent, our uncertain position in the district and at the Board helped us. We had no "official" recognition as a school, and there were those who would have preferred to see us fail. We were not surrounded by enemies, exactly, but true friends were few. Protecting Central Park East and ensuring its continued existence was our responsibility, and that served, I think, to persuade staff members to rethink grievances, moderate language, and put self-interest a little to the side. However strong our differences, we managed to work them out among ourselves, and while many of us were strong unionists, we never found it necessary to use formal grievance procedures to settle conflicts.

We still operate in this improvisational, open-ended, somewhat messy way. We do solve problems and resolve issues, but it's never quite clear to me how we have managed it. All of our directors—Deborah Meier, Lucy Matos, and most recently Jane Andrias—have been quite different in their styles of leadership, yet each has been able to provide the support we need to sustain our work.

A close, personal, intense relationship with students is inevitable when you see them as singular and special, and not just as this year's "class." The danger is that all the caring and intensity can lead to the creation of a pious, self-righteous, hothouse instead of a good school. Our continuing struggles to stay true to some ideal of community serve to keep the intensity in check, and regularly forces each of us out of the classroom and into the public spaces of our public school.

The quality of relationships between teachers and students is a recurring theme in the graduates' stories. Some connections were closer than others since staff members and families were personal friends. But few children at Central Park East ever felt anonymous or invisible. In fact, the reverse is probably true: We sometimes worried that there was too *little* opportunity for children to enjoy the pleasures of solitude, the comfort of being unseen and unheard. One solution was to provide places where someone could go for a little "invisibility"—lofts, quiet corners, and "secret" enclosures where a child who chose to could be quite alone.

The CPE staff has always been a diverse, strong-minded, opinionated lot. We did not have a systematic, formal philosophy. Our work was based on a set of shared beliefs, loose enough to accommodate diversity but with a strong central core. We believed that school was supposed to be exciting and interesting, and we had a responsibility to make it that way. Most children liked to cook, for example, so that was a regular part of every day's activity in most classrooms. When necessary, it could be justified as "experiential" math. But the real reason, in my classroom as least, was that the cooks had a good time doing it and the rest of us enjoyed gobbling the results. Every winter, when the rink in Central Park opened, we took all our classes ice skating. For the record, it was a component of our phys ed program, but for the children, it was simply great fun, and an experience some of us otherwise would never have had. These things did not happen in very many public schools then and the practice is not common now. Who has time for fun when there are workbook pages to be filled, curriculum covered, textbooks read, and standardized tests taken and retaken, year after year?

Another belief about teaching and learning was that one had to know what a youngster cared about in order to support and sustain that interest in the classroom. The challenge was greatest with children who showed little interest in the activities available or the possibilities we suggested, but we made the assumption that every child cared about something and we needed to help him or her discover what it was. One year, a small group of boys was serious about boats. While others drew jet planes, they drew battleships, aircraft carriers, landing barges. The interest had been evident during the previous year, so I designed a special curriculum just for them. They learned about boats, made models, conducted sinking and floating experiments, climbed aboard the *Peking* at the South Street Seaport, imagined themselves cabin boys on a sailing ship, and wrote imaginary diaries. They read and wrote about boats and painted seascapes. Their enthusiasm was contagious; others joined in. We performed *HMS Pinafore* as the class play.

The deep engagement with children was not a theoretical construct, but an inevitable and necessary component of our work. We had to figure out how to teach what children wanted or needed to learn. It couldn't be done if we didn't know and understand each child. We had, after all, dispensed with formal curriculum and were inventing our own, based on what we observed in the classroom and insights we gained through watching kids, thinking about the choices they made, and working with them.

I wonder how many regular students, in ordinary classrooms, feel recognized and visible in this way. I'm sure the "smart" ones do, and the "bad" ones, of course, but what about the others, the ones who don't stand out for any particular reason? It seems to me that at Central Park East, we had our share of "standouts" of both kinds. But many of the rest of our students would have been the nearly invisible, "good" kids of a typical school, unremarked and unremarkable. At our school, I like to think, we tried to make sure *everybody* was noticed, that every child was the center of some circle, no matter how small its circumference.

I have taught close to 600 children at Central Park East. By rights, I should have forgotten some of them by now, especially those I taught during my early years at the school. I'm famous for my terrible memory and general absent-mindedness, so a little "slippage" would not be surprising. Yet, I remember every single one. (I contrast that collection of memories, somewhat sadly, with the mostly forgotten names and faces of the children I taught for 12 years at another school before moving to CPE. I worked hard at that school, thought and taught to the best of my ability; I know I cared, but I didn't *notice* much, so few stand out.) I must admit that I can't always put a name to a face in the very first moments or see the youngster I knew in the smiling adult who shakes my hand or gives me a hug. But, inevitably, I notice a gesture, hear an inflection, catch a smile, and the child I knew as a fifth or sixth grader pops up.

I was an experienced, energetic, enthusiastic teacher when I began at CPE but not, I think, an outstanding one. David Bensman characterizes us as a group of practitioners who "learned how to learn" and accurately describes the sources and results of that knowledge building. But there is a critical dimension that he's missed. It wasn't only progressive pedagogy, Deborah Meier's leadership, training at the City College Workshop Center, and using the Prospect processes and all the rest of the things I "learned" that transformed me into an accomplished teacher. All of it was important, of course, but I believe I was able to flourish and *become* a good teacher because I was not only encouraged but expected to try out new ideas in a setting where it was reasonably safe to "make mistakes." It was one of Debbie's best ideas, one that was essential for my growth, at least. She persuaded me that taking risks and making mistakes was as necessary for us as teachers as it was for our students, and that I was not doing irreparable damage to kids by trying out ideas that didn't work. In fact, "playing with ideas" was the language we used to describe what we wanted children to do. "Mucking about" was another favorite phrase, borrowed from our British Infant School coreligionists. As a result, some of the work I did with children was exciting and rich and intellectually challenging, but some was flimsy and embarrassingly superficial. (Oh, those cardboard-box dollhouses!) I worried about the children who couldn't make choices, who didn't have the deep interest, self-discipline, or thoughtfulness needed to follow through on projects and produce good work. I worried that my teaching was not of high quality; I was uncertain about how to formulate standards and apply them.

Talking with Debbie or with other staff members was always reassuring: Someone else was bound to have a concern similar to mine or, even when different, equally worrisome. Often, talking to a student's former teacher and reading through her or his collection of narrative reports put things into perspective. It was important to know that it wasn't just in *my* room that Dorothy was disinterested or evasive or angry with everyone. Equally important was the understanding that I was never "stuck" with something that wasn't working. I could change the curriculum, the room arrangement, the work schedule. These were not impulsive, whimsical changes. I was not introducing novelty for its own sake, but because things weren't going as I wanted them to. Children were not enjoying the curriculum and neither was I. It had been a bad idea so the only thing to do was wrap it up quickly, pack up what was worth saving, move on, and plan more carefully the next time.

Obviously, there was always a next time, always another opportunity to try things again, correct mistakes, polish off the rough bits, add some new ingredients. The truth is that no matter what the curriculum, I invariably find myself mentally revising it for its next appearance, even as I'm very much doing it in the here and now. New ideas present themselves as each new group of students tries things out, generates fresh perspectives, points up weaknesses, shows me what I have missed, forgotten, or never knew. This way of working is personal style. I'm not good at visualizing; I have to put the furniture in place (and move it around half a dozen times) to know whether it will work. Doing and redoing curriculum and documenting as I go along also serves as a method of self-study. It helps me figure things out, see what I'm learning, identify errors and failures.

It's ironic, I think, but not surprising, that while the CPE staff was "inventing" this new, interesting school and laboring mightily to create a curriculum and pedagogy that would offer choice, challenge, and academic rigor, our students were attending to something else. Their most intense memories are of friendships. Of course, some speak about the intellectual content of their education at Central Park East, grateful for the ideas they encountered as well as their rich experiences with the arts. They acknowledge the academic rigor of the work they were asked to do and the standards to which they were held. Others recognize how hard teachers worked to support their strengths and find alternative ways to teach what was "hard" for them to learn. But what really mattered was what they learned about friendship, and what they learned because they were among friends. Despite our uncertainties about how to create the right kind of school culture, we were successful, it seems, in supporting children's connections to one another, helping them sort through issues of race and class and ethnicity, and clearing the common ground so that there could be a place on it for everyone. In short, we helped them make sense of the social world as well as the phenomenal one.

The language we used, especially in the early days of the school, was of the CPE family. It was meant to represent a public space large enough to hold us all—children, parents, extended families, staff—and to encourage a vision of a school world that went beyond the formal and traditional. Of course, being who we were, participation in CPE family life was very much a matter of individual choice, for families as well as staff. Some families, through all their years with us, maintained some degree of formality and distance; others established strong personal ties with individual staff members that lasted long beyond graduation day. Some staff members have become lifelong friends. This collection of relationships, complex and nuanced, is how children experienced friendships among the adults they knew as teachers and sometimes as friends and colleagues of their parents. They learned that valuing and respecting one another was one of the things that mattered a lot at CPE.

For too many young people, school is about things that don't matter or that are so painful they are best forgotten. I teach a class in the philosophy of education at Brooklyn College. The first assignment asks students to write about their school experiences. I am troubled and saddened by what I read. They remember so little of what they learned or did in elementary or middle school. One or two individuals describe a special moment or a particularly gifted teacher, but the majority of stories are painful ones about cruelty, humiliation, and failure. There is the rare description of a teacher who had the capacity to challenge and excite students; even more uncommon is one who noticed a talent or interest or ability and made special efforts to nurture it.

Our vision of schooling was never a fixed and final thing, but we wanted to help every student find a special talent, or interest, or serious passion. We looked together, supported what we found, tried to sustain and nourish it. But it's impossible to know which particular aspects of the complex, adult person I see now, was shaped by some piece of work she or he did in the fifth grade. I would love it if some graduate were to say, "Alice, I hungered to be a writer and you recognized it and showed me the way." That's the movie version; real learning isn't like that.

Unlike my college students, the graduates of Central Park East remember school as being about things that mattered: freedom and friendships, choices and challenges. Their teachers seemed to be saying, "Let's find out what you care about." It went beyond reading a particular book, painting a particular picture, or having a particular friend.

These things happened in some way for all the children. We were after something larger: It's important for you to know what matters, because once you discover what that is, you can do something with it, for yourself or for others.

It's what school is really about; we could call it learning by heart.

Alice Seletsky
January 1996

New York City Elementary Public School Students as a Comparison Group

COMPARISON OF THE RACIAL composition of the CPE and the New York City public school population reveals that CPE's population contained far more children of color, and far fewer Whites, than did the New York City public school population as a whole (see Table A.1).

All groups of CPE students had high school graduation rates that compared favorably with the citywide figures. This was especially true for Hispanic and African American students, but it was true for White students as well (see Table A.2).

This comparison actually represents an underestimation of CPE's efficacy, for the citywide data summarize information about all students who *began ninth grade* in New York City public high schools, *not all those who graduated from sixth grade.* Thus, the citywide figures exclude those who left school before entering ninth grade, while the CPE figures include all sixth-grade graduates.

Furthermore, while the data on family income of the New York City population and CPE students are not fully comparable, they suggest that

Table A.1. New York City Elementary Public School Population and CPE Population by Race, 1978-1983 (percent)

	New York City	CPE
Caucasian	25.7	11.6
Asian	4.5	0.0
Black	36.3	57.0
Hispanic	33.5	31.4
American Indian	< 0.1	0.0

Sources: U.S. Department of Education, Office of Civil Rights, *Annual Ethnic Census*, 1985; CPE survey, available from author.
Note: New York City percentages total over 100 due to rounding.

Table A.2. High School Graduation Rates of CPE Graduates and Citywide Population by Race, 1987 (percent)

	New York City	CPE
All	66.9	94.8
African American	66.9	95.7
Hispanic	57.6	92.1
White	73.5	100.0

Sources: New York City, Office of Research, Evaluation and Assessment, *The Cohort Report*, 1990; 1991 survey of CPE graduates, 1978-1983.

Notes: CPE graduates include those receiving high school diplomas or GEDs. Citywide high school graduation rates are based on a cohort study of 1986-87 high school graduates, which included those graduating from CPE in 1981.

more CPE students came from poor families than was true of the city population as a whole (see Table A.3).

Another way to compare the CPE cohort with that of the city as a whole is to compare the composition of the families in which students were raised. Such a comparison reveals that the family structure of New York City families containing children under the age of 18 and that of CPE families was rather similar, although the proportion of CPE graduates living in families headed by a single mother was higher than that for the city as a whole (see Table A.4).

Finally, comparisons of data on mothers' occupations show that the proportion of mothers of CPE graduates in "managerial/professional jobs" was higher than the proportion of all New York City women in such jobs (see Table A.5), although changes over time (citywide data are as of 1980, compared with 1991 for CPE graduates) may to some extent be a confounding factor here.

Table A.3. Family Income of New York City Population and CPE Students

Income Level	New York City (%)	CPE (%)
1980 Dollars		
Under $10,000	29.4	
$10,000-$15,000	56.2	
$15,000 and above	14.4	
1985 Dollars		
Under $12,000		50.0
$12,000-$20,000		25.0
Above $20,000		25.0

Sources: U.S. Bureau of the Census, *Twentieth Census of the United States*, 1980; CPE survey, available from author.

Note: The high inflation rate during 1980-1985 means that an income of $12,000 in 1985 was equivalent to an income of $10,000 in 1980.

Table A.4. Family Structure of New York City Population and CPE Graduates (percent of families with persons under 18 years old)

Family Type	New York City	CPE
Householder or spouse	0.2	0.0
Own child		
Married couple	58.0	61.5
Female householder	30.9	36.6
Other	11.1	1.9

Sources: U.S. Bureau of the Census, *Twentieth Census of the United States,* 1980; CPE survey, available from author.
Notes: New York city values are as of 1980; CPE values are as of 1991. New York City percentages total over 100 due to rounding.

Table A.5. Occupation of Mother, New York City Population and CPE Graduates (percent of employed mothers)

	New York City	CPE
Managerial/Professional	24.5	31.3
Tech./Sales/Admin. Support	48.7	47.4
Precision Production/Crafts	1.9	0.0
Operator/Fabricator/Laborer	10.5	0.0
Service	14.3	21.3

Sources: U.S. Bureau of the Census, *Twentieth Census of the United States,* 1980; CPE survey, available from author.
Notes: New York City values are as of 1980; CPE values are as of 1991. New York City percentages do not total 100 due to rounding.

Alice Seletsky's Reports on Valerie Sanchez

I. Projects, Themes, Interests

February 1983: This has been a very busy and productive time for Valerie. She's been working hard at everything and has been actively involved with many different projects. She's continuing her work with Laurie in the pottery room. Two mornings a week, she works with Jane Andrias, who is our art teacher this year. Valerie's artwork is quite lovely; she has a real sense of design, color, and composition. Jane has been teaching the group some techniques for drawing and painting; how to draw figures in motion; proportions of the human body; how to draw faces. Valerie has been working in different media—pencil, charcoal, paint, tissue paper—and has done still-life sketches and paintings, work on a mural, lots of drawing and collage. In the coming weeks, she'll be doing some studies of portraits and how different artists have painted them. In all her work, Valerie shows a concern for detail, high standards, and the ability to work in a very concentrated way. The work she produces is very, very good, and she has a definite talent for art.

She's worked on other things as well. Early in the term, she did a piece of weaving, copying an original design that she made on graph paper. In connection with our study of the ancient Middle East, she made a model of a Palestinian tomb which was accurate and realistic. She's done lots of good writing, made her own adaptation of the story of Joseph and his brothers, and has been working on a series of science experiments and explorations.

June 1983: This has been a busy and productive time for Valerie. She began collecting stories and poems from other children in the class for a magazine, which she and K. wanted to publish. They got pretty far along with it, but it never quite got finished.

Science was an interest for a while, and Valerie did a series of experiments about oxygen, evaporation, heat, fermentation, making carbon and carbon dioxide. She is an organized thinker and methodical worker. She also has perseverance—when an experiment doesn't work the first time, she is quite willing to repeat it until it does yield results that make sense.

Valerie is a talented artist and works hard at painting, drawing, and working with clay. She has done many different kinds of paintings and learned several different techniques. She helped plan, design, and paint some of the scenery for our class play, *The Pirates of Penzance*. The sets were wonderful, and Valerie certainly deserves some of the credit.

I know she enjoyed acting in the play, too. Her acting was wonderful—she had confidence and spontaneity, and communicated a real sense of herself and her role to the audience. During rehearsals, she was always patient and helpful, helped other children memorize their parts, and did all she could to help things go smoothly. She made a genuine contribution to the success of the show.

II. The following issues, which we have discussed in conferences, cover important aspects of your child as a learner, and as a member of the school community. We've used the following code:

(1) A serious problem that will continue to need our attention
(2) Needs improvement—lots of reminders—but is coming along
(3) All's well
(4) A major area of strength

3   Homework
3   Attendance
3   Punctuality
3   Ability to handle classroom routines
3   Helpfulness in maintaining classroom environment
4   Relationship with classmates   3   with adults
3   Focus, attentiveness to work; study habits
4   Responsibility in carrying out assignments
3   Cooperation and service to larger school community

III. Reading Assessment

CPE Reading Code:

0   Pre-reading
1   Beginning reading (copies, pretends, recognizes familiar words)
2   Early reading (simple, repetitive books, easy vocabulary)
3   Minimum literacy (basic vocabulary, some independence)

4 Basic literacy (can read anything, but it's still "work")
5 Full fluency (reads silently and with ease)

Comments

February 1983: Valerie is a completely fluent reader, and I suspect that, at this point, there's very little material written for children of her age and grade level, which she can't read. She sometimes has trouble with interpreting factual information—things she reads in the encyclopedia, for example. This is partly due, I think, to inexperience with this kind of reading matter. Valerie has read lots of stories, but very little nonfiction. One of the things I want her to begin doing, during this latter part of the term, is reading nonfiction books, like biographies, books on science subjects, and current affairs.

In the classroom, Valerie has read so many books that a complete list would take several pages. Here is a small sample: many Nancy Drew mysteries, chapter books like *Sadako and the Thousand Paper Cranes*, simplified versions of classics like *Jane Eyre, Oliver Twist,* and *The Adventures of Robin Hood.*

June 1983: Valerie is a fluent reader. She scored above average on the reading test we gave this spring. She loves books and reads for recreation as well as information. Titles of books read recently:

Silver Eyes
Why Doesn't She Go Home?
Quest of the Missing Map

Writing:

February 1983: Valerie is a very good writer. The stories in her journal are carefully planned and constructed. She's beginning to be able to read her own work critically and to revise and rewrite parts that don't satisfy her. This is difficult for most children to do, but Valerie knows how to go about it, and she's a good judge of her work. Her story, *The Creature,* is an example of how she handles the process of editing and revising, and it's also a good example of the kind of writing she's capable of doing. The story has a clear plot, many effective details; the language is varied, and the ideas expressed clearly in properly constructed sentences. I liked the description of the creature who comes out of the space ship. It's clear, both from this piece of writing and her journal, that Valerie has mastered most of the mechanics of writing—punctuation, capitalization, paragraphing, grammar, and usage.

Valerie's research report on Mesopotamia was a little disappointing. It was adequate, but not the best work she's able to do. We talked about this, and I think Valerie agrees. The whole report was too short and didn't have enough detailed information. It also didn't have many interesting ideas and interpretations that were Valerie's own. Since I know what Valerie's capabilities are, I have no doubt that the next report will be up to her usual high standards.

Math:

February 1983: Valerie is an excellent math student, and she's been making very good progress. On the test that we gave last November, Valerie demonstrated that she can work confidently and accurately with all the mathematical concepts that are considered appropriate to her grade. She is working in the E2 book of the CDA series and will finish in the next few weeks and go on to the F1 book.

Valerie is able to do all kinds of computation with fractions. She can find prime factors of a number through constructing factor trees. She's been doing a lot of work with percentages and ratios and is coming to understand them. In addition, she's learned a lot of geometry—area and perimeter of polygons, circumferences of circles, and measuring angles. In the weeks to come, we'll be concentrating on computation with decimal numbers, exponential notation, negative numbers, and number systems other than base ten.

June 1983: Valerie is an excellent math student. She scored well above average in the math test that we gave this spring. She is able to do the following:

> read and interpret numbers in the millions and higher
> round off whole numbers to the nearest hundred, thousand, etc.
> estimate an answer before computing
> identify prime numbers
> construct a factor tree and find prime factors
> find the common multiple of a set of numbers
> find area and perimeter of rectangles
> measure angles, using a protractor
> find the circumference of a circle

Bibliography

Asher, S., & Gottman, J. (Eds.). (1981). *The development of children's friendships.* Cambridge: Cambridge University Press.

Ayers, W. (1993). *To teach: The journey of a teacher.* New York: Teachers College Press.

Beer, M., Eisenstat, R., & Spector, B. (1990). *The critical path to corporate renewal.* Cambridge, MA: Harvard Business School Press.

Bensman, D. (1987). *Quality education in the inner city: The story of the Central Park East School.* New York: Center for Collaborative Education.

Bensman, D. (1994). *Lives of the graduates of the Central Park East Elementary School: What did they do? What did they learn?* New York: NCREST.

Burbules, N. C., & Rice, S. (1991, November). Dialogue across differences: Continuing the conversation. *Harvard Educational Review, 61,* 393–415.

Bussis, A. (1985). *Inquiry into meaning: An investigation of learning to read.* Hillsdale, NJ: Erlbaum.

Carter, K. (1993, January–February). The place of story in the study of teaching and teacher education. *Educational Researcher,* pp. 5–12.

Clark, R. M. (1983). *Family life and school achievement.* Chicago: University of Chicago Press.

Comer, J. (1988, January). Is "parenting" essential to good teaching? *NEA Journal,* pp. 34–40.

Cremin, L. A. (1964). *The transformation of the school: Progressivism in American education, 1876–1957.* New York: Vintage Books.

Cullen, C. L. (1991). *Middle College High School: Its organization and effectiveness.* Unpublished dissertation, Teachers College, Columbia University, New York.

Darling-Hammond, L. (1993, June). Reframing the school reform agenda: Developing capacity for school transformation. *Phi Delta Kappan,* pp. 753–761.

Darling-Hammond, L., & Goodwin, A. L. (1993). Progress toward professionalism in teaching. In G. Cawelti (Ed.), *Challenges and achievements of American education* (pp. 23–28). Alexandria, VA: Association for Supervision and Curriculum Development.

Delpit, L. D. (1988, August). The silenced dialogue: Power and pedagogy in educating other people's children. *Harvard Educational Review, 3,* 280–298.

Delpit, L. D. (1992). Education in a multicultural society: Our future's greatest challenge. *Journal of Negro Education, 61*(3), 237–249.

147

Dropkin, R., & Tobier, A. (Eds.). (1976). *Roots of open education in America*. New York: City College Workshop Center for Open Education.

Fine, G. A. (1981). Friends, impression management, and preadolescent behavior. In S. R. Asher & J. M. Gottman (Eds.), *The development of children's friendships* (pp. 29–53). Cambridge: Cambridge University Press.

Fiske, E. B. (1992). *Smart schools, smart kids*. New York: Simon & Schuster.

Fitzgerald, L. M., & Goncu, A. (1993). Parent involvement in urban childhood education: A Vygotskian approach. In S. Reifel (Ed.), *Advances in early education and day care: A research annual* (pp. 447–452). Greenwich, CT: JAI Press.

Fliegel, S., & MacGuire, J. (1993). *Miracle in East Harlem: The fight for choice in public education*. New York: Times Books.

Frank, D. B. (1983). *Deep blue funk and other stories: Portraits of teenage parents*. Chicago: University of Chicago Press.

Gray, P., & Chanoff, D. (1986, February). Democratic schooling: What happens to young people who have charge of their own education? *American Journal of Education, 85*, 182–213.

Greene, M. (1993, January–February). The passions of pluralism: Multiculturalism and the expanding community. *Educational Researcher*, pp. 13–19.

Heckscher, C., & Donnellon, A. (Eds.). (1994). *The post-bureaucratic organization: New perspectives on organizational change*. Thousand Oaks, CA: Sage.

Howard, R. (Ed.). (1993). *The learning imperative: Managing people for continuous innovation*. Cambridge, MA: Harvard Business Review Press.

Institute for Education in Transformation. (1993). *Voices from the inside: A report on schooling from inside the classroom*. Claremont Graduate School, Claremont, CA.

Jervis, K., & Montag, C. (Eds.). (1991). *Progressive education for the 1990s: Transforming practice*. New York: Teachers College Press.

Jervis, K., & Tobier, A. (Eds.). (1987). *Education for democracy*. Cambridge School, Cambridge, MA.

Kohl, H. (1991). *I won't learn from you*. Minneapolis: Milkweed.

Kozol, J. (1990). *The night is dark and I am far from home*. New York: Simon & Schuster.

Lamar, J. (1991). *Bourgeois blues: An American memoir*. New York: Summit Books.

Lieberman, A. (Ed.). (1990). *Schools as collaborative cultures: Creating the future now*. New York: Falmer Press.

Lowe, R., & Miner, B. (1992). False choices: Why school vouchers threaten our children's future. *Rethinking Schools, 6* (3), 21–23. Milwaukee.

Meier, D. (1995). *The power of their ideas*. Boston: Beacon Press.

Minuchin, P., Biber, B., Shapiro, E., & Zimiles, H. (1969). *The psychological impact of school experience: A comparative study of nine-year old children in contrasting schools*. New York: Basic Books.

Nelson, J. L., Palonsky, S. B., & Carlson, K. (1990). *Critical issues in education*. New York: McGraw-Hill.

Nickerson, R. S. (1988–89). On improving thinking through instruction. *Review of Research in Education, 15*, 3–57.

Noddings, N. (1992). *The challenge to care in schools: An alternative approach to education*. New York: Teachers College Press.

Nonoka, I. (1988, Spring). Toward middle-up-down management: Accelerating information creation. *Sloan Management Review, 30*(9), 9–18.

Office of Research, Evaluation, and Assessment. (1990). *The cohort report: Four-year results for the class of 1989 and follow-ups of the classes of 1986, 1987, and 1988.* New York City Board of Education.

Peskin, A. (1991). *The color of strangers, the color of friends: The play of ethnicity in school and community.* Chicago: University of Chicago Press.

Ravitch, D., & Goodenow, R. K. (1981). *Educating an urban people: The New York City experience.* New York: Teachers College Press.

Raywid, M. A. (1985, Winter). Family choice arrangements. *Review of Educational Research, 55*(4), 435–467.

Rose, M. (1995). *Possible lives.* Boston: Houghton Mifflin.

Rothstein, R. (1993, Spring). The myth of public school failure. *The American Prospect,* pp. 20–34.

Schofield, J. W. (1981). Complementary and conflicting identities: Images and interaction in an interracial school. In S. R. Asher & J. M. Gottman (Eds.), *The development of children's friendships* (pp. 53–90). Cambridge: Cambridge University Press.

Schofield, J. W. (1989). *Black and white in school: Trust, tension, or tolerance.* New York: Teachers College Press.

Sharp, R., & Green, A., with Lewis, J. (1975). *Education and social control: A study in progressive primary education.* London: Routledge & Kegan Paul.

Silberman, C. (1970). *Crisis in the classroom: The remaking of American education.* New York: Random House.

Snyder, J., Lieberman, A., Macdonald, M., & Goodwin, A. L. (1992). *Makers of meaning in a learning-centered school: A case study of Central Park East I Elementary School.* New York: NCREST.

Sosniak, L. A. (1987, Summer). The nature of change in successful learning. *Teachers College Record, 88*(4), 519–536.

Sosniak, L. A. (1990). The tortoise, the hare, and the development of talent. In M. J. A. Howe (Ed.), *Encouraging the development of exceptional skills and talents* (pp. 149–164). Leicester, England: BPS Books.

Steinitz, V. A., & Solomon, E. R. (1987). *Starting out: Class and community in the lives of working-class youth.* Philadelphia: Temple University Press.

Tainsh, P. (1994). *Central Park East Elementary Schools: Social benefit analysis study.* New York: Bruner Foundation.

Taylor, D. (1988). *Growing up literate: Learning from inner-city families.* Portsmouth, NH: Heinemann.

Weiner, L. (1993). *Preparing teachers for urban schools: Lessons from thirty years of school reform.* New York: Teachers College Press.

Wood, G. H. (1992). *Schools that work: America's most innovative public education programs.* New York: Dutton.

Index

152

About the Author

DAVID BENSMAN teaches in the Department of Labor Studies and Employment Relations of the School of Management and Labor Relations at Rutgers University. He is the author of *The Practice of Solidarity: American Hat Finishers in the Nineteenth Century*, and co-author (with Roberta Lynch) of *Rusted Dreams: Hard Times in a Steel Community*. He was also one of the co-authors of volume 2 of *Who Built America?* In addition to writing on labor history and labor relations, Professor Bensman has written several studies on education and school reform, including *Quality Education in the Inner-City*, and three monographs published by the National Center for Restructuring Education, Schools and Teaching (NCREST), including *Lives of the Graduates of the Central Park East School*, *Learning to Think Well*, and *Building a Family-School Partnership in a Bronx Elementary School*. The last is part of the NCREST Series on Cultural Interchange.